TARTINE BREAD

TARTINE BREAD

by Chad Robertson

photographs by Eric Wolfinger

CHRONICLE BOOKS

SAN FRANCISCO

Text copyright © 2010 by Chad Robertson.

Photographs copyright © 2010 by Eric Wolfinger and Chad Robertson.

Library of Congress Cataloging-in-Publication Data available.

ISBN 978-0-8118-7041-2

Manufactured in China

Designed by **VANESSA DINA**.
Food and prop styling by **ERIC WOLFINGER** and **CHAD ROBERTSON**.
Typesetting by **JANIS REED**.
Photograph on page 29 by Catherine Karnow.
Front cover image and photographs on pages 19, 34, 35, 78, 115, 136, 138, 150, 178, 210, 216, 222, 224, 236, 239, and 252 by Chad Robertson.
Photographs on pages 18 and 42 by Suzanne Yacovetti.
Illustrations by David Wilson.
Page 9: *Les Canotiers de la Meurthe,* Émile Friant, 1888.
Courtesy of Le Musée de l'École de Nancy.

10 9

Chronicle Books LLC
680 Second Street
San Francisco, California 94107
WWW.CHRONICLEBOOKS.COM

For Archer and Elisabeth

TABLE OF CONTENTS

Bread in Time 8

CHAPTER 1
Basic Country Bread 41

CHAPTER 2
Semolina and Whole-Wheat Breads 109

CHAPTER 3
Baguettes and Enriched Breads 123

CHAPTER 4
Days-Old Bread 175

Acknowledgments 295

Index 297

Table of Equivalents 304

Bread in Time

My strongest inspiration came not from real bread but from images—images of a time and place when bread was the foundation of a meal and at the center of daily life. There is a painting of boaters gathered at a riverside table. At the head, a large crusty loaf held close to the heart is cut into wedges to commence the meal. This scene was painted a little more than a century ago in France, when a worker's portion of bread was two pounds per day, and bread was on every table at mealtime. This was elemental bread that sustained generations. To find this bread, I would have to learn make it. Thus began my search for a certain loaf with an old soul.

I opened my first bakery nearly fifteen years ago after three years of formal apprenticeship and with the vision of my ideal loaf taking shape. Each loaf would tell the hands of the baker who made it, and each would also have its own expression—like a clay vessel pulled from the kiln after firing. The loaf would be baked dark, and the substantial, blistered crust would hold some give while containing a voluptuous, wildly open crumb with the sweet character of natural fermentation and a subtle balanced acidity. The bread would be a joy to eat fresh and would keep well for a week.

Although I had apprenticed with some of the finest artisan bakers in the United States and France, none had taught me how to make the loaf I was envisioning. Instead, they gave me the tools to get there.

From my first mentor, I learned to approach bread making as both a craft and a philosophy of ingredients and how they interact. With that understanding came the promise that I could find my way to any bread I imagined. "Dough is dough," he liked to say, implying that all breads are closely related—even the ones that seemed quite different.

After years of learning, I realized I would never get there working under the tutelage of someone else. I was twenty-three when Elisabeth, now my wife, and I built our first small bakeshop with the help of friends north of San Francisco, along the coast of Tomales Bay. Bakeshop was an apt name for the room where I would spend the next six years working. We cut a hole in the wall and built a wood-fired oven outside facing into the shop. The shop was one step from the home where we lived. Technically, I was a home baker with a big oven. I would have to make hundreds of loaves a day for years in a sort of solitary baking trance to achieve what I had in my mind's eye.

I started with the wood-fired oven and no mixer. The rigor of mixing three hundred pounds of dough by hand required a softer dough, so I added more water.

During my first apprenticeship, I had worked with wet doughs, so this was familiar territory. The oven was fired all day as the dough was mixed, shaped, and set to rise on cloths. The loaves were ready to bake a few hours after shaping, and I baked through the night. But after months with little sleep, I changed my course. Opening the windows in the evening cooled the dough down and slowed the final rising significantly. The bake could wait until the next morning.

I held close to my ideal, but after such a long rise, the resulting bread was sometimes more sour than I wanted. To counter this, I began using my wild yeast starter at a younger, more mild stage until I achieved the complex flavors I was after with the right balance of acidity. Now, I could get a decent night's rest, freed from the "life of bats." The only problem with this new schedule was that I would have to bake later in the day and sell bread in the afternoon. So that's what I did: gaining the pleasures of warm bread for dinner and toast for breakfast. After a decade of working alone, I took on my first apprentices. I had spent almost half my life obsessing over bread; it was now something I did, not something I talked about. Making bread had become a mostly silent meditation for me, and I liked it that way. It would take a fortuitous trade agreement to draw me out.

In 2005, Eric Wolfinger came to work at Tartine with no baking experience. He was on track to becoming a chef before he decided to try his hand at baking. Eric grew up surfing in Southern California and noticed that I had an ideal surfing schedule: starting my day around noon and finishing in the early evening. He suggested a trade. He offered to teach me to surf, and I would teach him to make bread. Eric's persistence wore me down, and I agreed to try surfing.

By the time my sore ribs had healed from my first surfing session, I had a new obsession, and he was the one to talk to. He followed my every surfing question with another question about bread. During those long drives up and down the coast, we often had two conversations going on at once. Months and years passed as we learned together, surfing in the morning and baking in the afternoon.

Lucky for me, Eric stuck around long enough to learn to make great bread, gaining the keen understanding of my approach that would make our collaboration on this book possible.

Over the course of time, I articulated what had been only in my head and redefined for myself the craft of bread making. The idea was to distill the content of our daily discussions into techniques that would work well for the home baker—to make a baker's guidebook.

Traditional, intuitive bread making does not lend itself naturally to a written recipe. Before the study of microbiology, bakers understood the subtleties of the process. The nature of fermentation was second nature to their own. That is, they understood fermentation in relation to the rhythms of their own lives. It

is necessarily the same with modern artisan bakers. All points lead back to the starter and the leaven as origin of the process, and the way that they are used to manage fermentation determines the outcome. Then, as now, the most important aspect of making bread was managing the stages of fermentation by knowing what to look for. The visual element would be an integral part of this book project. There was no question in my mind that Eric had to document our work. He was uniquely qualified by his experience, his daily baking shift, and his passion for photography. *Tartine Bread* would have to be photographed throughout the process of building the book. This would require another year's commitment from Eric.

When I started describing how to make the basic loaf, I knew it would take some work to translate my method into a process for making something comparable at home. Eric had been baking on his days off at home for years, using a cast-iron combo cooker as a baking vessel with excellent results. He suggested we set up a private blog for a handful of bread testers, send them all combo cookers, and engage in a virtual dialogue—sharing photos of home-baked bread, answering questions, and adding to our instructions where they needed more clarity.

Mostly, I expected it would be a helpful progress check, as we initially intended to post every recipe for testing as we completed it. But within the first week, we discovered two things: there were not enough hours in the day for us to maintain an interactive blog, and many of our test bakers achieved, in their first attempt, bread at home that looked as if it had come out of our own ovens on a good day. We had expected neither of these things, but the latter was a revelation. Indeed, the exemplary bread we show in the first chapter is a home-baked tester loaf.

We stayed in contact with a few of the bread testers, who continued to bake regularly. We answered questions as the testers came up with their own schedules, modifying times and temperatures so that making bread fit into their lives. Some made breads that were close to the original mold, while others made different, equally delicious breads to suit their needs and their vision.

This was exactly what we had hoped for, and I decided to profile some of our testers in this book. Relating our testers' real-life experiences, I discuss how they altered our approach to get distinctly different breads.

The "Tartine Bread" approach follows a loose set of concepts that we introduce in a single "basic recipe" and then build on throughout the book. As you gain an understanding of how bread "works," you will be able to make adjustments in timing and technique to achieve a broad range of results. The goal of making bread with a satisfying depth of flavor, a good crust, and a moist, supple crumb is a constant.

We begin by showing you how to make a leaven and then how to make our Tartine Basic Country Bread at home. Since bread making has always been a visual learning experience for me, I wanted a heavily photographic depiction of

the process to start. Jacques Pepin's books *La Technique* and *La Méthode* were strong inspirations. Learning a craft is as much about copying as it is about understanding, as much visual as it is intellectual. As an apprentice, I watched bakers making bread and then cleaned up after them. Eventually I got my hands in the dough. Here you'll do both.

We explored the notion of starting the book with a yeasted bread recipe to encourage those who might be intimidated by beginning with a wild yeast starter. We reasoned that if the rise was long and slow, we would get something respectable to start with, and then dive into making a natural leaven for a more challenging but rewarding loaf. We found that the difference in the time it takes to make a well-fermented yeasted bread and a natural leavened one was negligible. But the difference in quality was considerable. The straight yeasted bread lacked everything we love about the original. It simply did not have the savor or the staying power.

Tartine Bread is devoted to the use of natural leaven, often called sourdough. I promote using a "younger" leaven with very little acidity. It's a sweet-smelling, yeastier relative of the more sour and vinegary-smelling sourdough. When making bread with nothing more than flour, water, and salt, aspiring bakers should apply their attention to learning how to control the process of fermentation. The concept is not without precedent.

Up until the 1930s, French bakers used natural leaven in bread, croissants, and brioche. After commercial yeast became available, the skilled practice of caring for and using natural leaven declined. Convenience gained the upper hand, and flavor was sacrificed. With this shift, the keystone in the tradition of baking was largely lost. Taste a brioche bread skillfully made with natural leaven and compare it to the straight-yeasted version. The substantial gains in savor, keeping qualities, and versatile uses with the natural leaven justify the time it takes to build and care for one. Once the natural leaven is thriving, you can use it any way that suits your taste and your schedule.

Beginning with the basic recipe, subsequent breads progress from the original, building on what you have learned in the previous recipes. All the bread recipes are based on one kilogram of flour, so you will be able to compare and contrast differences in ratios and effects in practice. By moving parts around slightly, shifting ratios, and adjusting handling, we show you how to move from the Tartine loaf to pizza and then to baguette, brioche, croissant, and English muffins. This is where you see the gears of the basic recipe in motion. Whether your ideal bread is a thin, crisp flatbread or a classic baguette, the basic recipe will remain "north." All variations are traced out from the basic country recipe, and the origins are traced back to it. This is a baking guidebook to get you where you want to go.

BOURDON

Tartine bread began in 1992, when I visited a bakery in the Berkshire Mountains of western Massachusetts a few months before graduating from the Culinary Institute of America in New York. On the way, I confided to Elisabeth Prueitt, my classmate at the time, the notion that I might want to become a bread baker.

Liz and I arrived late one morning while the bakers were deep into their shift. A modern interpretation of Satie echoed through the vast brick barn as the final loaves were pulled from the oven and packed into an overflowing delivery truck. The last baker on shift would make deliveries to surrounding towns.

This place seemed a better fit than the frenetic kitchens I had worked in before. The honest hand-craft and generous ambience struck a chord with my West Texas upbringing among generations of western boot and saddle makers.

While my culinary school classmates sought positions with well-known chefs in Manhattan, I settled on an apprenticeship with Richard Bourdon, a classically trained concert musician turned baker. Richard had quit the French horn to make bread in the late 1970s and packed his family for a tour (mostly on foot) of bakeries in the French Alps. When I met him in 1992, he was renowned as one of the first bakers in the United States to revive the use of a preindustrial French bread-making technique using extremely wet dough slowly risen with a wild yeast leaven. Richard's bread was notoriously difficult to prepare and had gained a cult following among the growing ranks of artisan bakers on the East Coast.

The affable baker accepted my request to apprentice on the spot, and offered Liz and me room and board in the farmhouse where he lived with his wife and five children. Liz began working as a pastry chef in a nearby restaurant, and I soon found myself working twelve-hour shifts for weeks. What I left in the evening, I would return to in the morning before sunrise. It was a long, hot summer working alone with Bourdon. We mixed, shaped, and pulled three thousand loaves a day from the oven, followed with a delivery route. I had found what would become my life's profession.

Richard's goal was to make "good food." He wanted to produce healthful bread, and for him that meant mixing the flour with enough water to hydrate and fully cook the starch to make it more digestible. "Try to cook a cup of rice in half a cup of water," he said to illustrate the point. He insisted on fermenting his dough with a wild yeast natural leaven over a long time because he believed the process unlocked the nutrition in whole grains that were otherwise indigestible. The resulting high hydration in combination with a long, natural fermentation created a distinctively delicious loaf of bread. Richard's bread was exceptionally moist and tender, and had a depth of flavor achieved only after a long, slow rise using natural leaven. His bread was indeed good food, but he could tell I was still searching. After two years, he encouraged me to move on and keep learning.

PROVENCE AND SAVOIE

Following a short stop in Northern California, Liz and I set off for the French Alps to find the baker about whom Richard had so often spoken. I was on the trail of my mentor's mentor. From stories Richard had told, my head was filled with visions of giant wood-fired ovens and a dough so wet it had to be shaped in midair before landing on the workbench. The Sorcerer's Apprentice came to mind. In reality, the broom would soon be in my hands, and I'd be sweeping the bakeshop every hour.

Though we did not camp in the forest on the outskirts of town as Richard had, we immersed ourselves in French provincial life—working first in Provence with Daniel Colin and then on to the Bauges Alpes range in the Savoie with Patrick LePort.

After meeting us at the train station when we arrived in Provence, Daniel found us a place to stay with a friend who owned an old wine château. The château had fallen into partial ruin surrounded by hectares of gnarled grapevines. He told us that there were a few people living on the property, and that it was now a *"naturaliste"* retreat. The château was called the *"marie fée,"* a new-age amalgam of Woodstock-era Americana, Sai Baba mysticism, and Provençal hillbilly.

We rode our bicycles through ancient vineyards and past shepherds on our way to the bakery each morning. Liz made pastry, working alongside the pâtissier, while I worked with the boulangers. Daniel took it upon himself to teach me the history of American jazz. His vinyl collection of Miles, Monk, Mingus, Coltrane, and Bill Evans was exhaustive. We lived on *pain intégrale*, jars of pâté, and local rosé wine, which was cheaper than water. It was a special time.

For the first few weeks, *l'americain* swept the shop and made rounds of instant coffee with hot tap water. Soon, though, my skills at the shaping table earned my acceptance. I realized how well prepared I was after working that hard season with Richard. The Frenchmen were surprised that I could properly handle their slack dough, which was common perhaps in the home-baking tradition but difficult to make on the larger production scale of a wholesale bakery. Available to cover shifts, I became an unexpected windfall in the ever-present logistical puzzle of scheduling vacation time in a French bakery while remaining open for business, and I fast found myself in the company of friends. We spent half a year at Daniel's Boulangerie Artisanale.

As we were readying to leave for the Alps, Daniel offered us a ride. He wanted to detour through Bordeaux to visit his aging father, and we had the time. The day we left, he made a small batch of bread specially for his father. It was a wetter dough than usual, with a long bulk rise, which he baked hot and dark. The crumb had huge pearlescent holes, and the crust cracked as it cooled. The bread seemed alive even as it cooled and settled. While he packed the bread for the journey, Daniel commented that "this is the way I'd always make bread for myself—but my customers would not buy it." It was radical bread—a study in extremes—and I was much closer to finding the loaf with an old soul.

The loaves that Daniel had baked for his father held strong in my mind. I had not seen bread like that anywhere before. Speeding west across France in his Peugeot turbo wagon filled with bread, he told me about a lone baker in a small village near the coast who made the same bread he had just made for his father.

The bakery was a one-room shop in the Mèdoc with a wood-fired oven and plank shelving on the wall for bread. A bell hung outside the door, and in the afternoon it was rung to signal that hot bread was being pulled from the oven—just in time for dinner. This turned the baking schedule I had known upside down. Fresh bread for dinner was perfectly ideal and why work all night to have fresh bread in the morning, when toast is a treat unto itself? Never getting his name, I always spoke of him as "the awesome baker." Years later, recalling him in desperation would help me find a livable schedule I had forgot existed.

On the way to the Savoie, Daniel also took me to meet Monsieur Voisin, the man who had designed and built Daniel and Patrick's stacked-deck wood-fired ovens, as well as rebuilding the centuries old oven of "the awesome baker." Though his name means "neighbor," *voisin* is the last word one might use to describe a man who had never traveled outside France and passionately despised foreigners. He enjoyed his own house-cured foie gras with a glass of Sauternes for breakfast and, inexplicably, invited us to join him. We ate *en plein air* next to a wooden rowboat planted thick with *fraises des bois*, while discussing French oven-building history.

Daniel dropped us off at Patrick LePort's bakery, Boulangerie Savoyarde, where we were received like family returning from travels. Alpine muesli and *petit épeautre*, locally grown spelt bread, sustained us, with the occasional raclette binge on off nights. The kindness and generosity of our hosts were humbling.

We loved the work, the food, and the afternoon hikes to visit nearby *alpages* where some of the bakers tended cows and goats at high elevation for making traditional regional, seasonal cheeses. Our fellow bakers had accepted us, and we began to settle in. We talked about staying, yet my French *copains* advised against it. They recognized my dedication as a young baker and told me to return to the States and build an oven to make my own bread. My time spent learning in France was essential and instructive, allowing me to place what Bourdon had taught me into a historical context of tradition.

In France at the time, apprentice bakers would work twenty years more before having the opportunity to open their own places. It was against generations of tradition for a young baker to strike out on his own. French bakers were constrained by traditions that bound them to make the types of bread people expected of them. A big loaf, baked dark with huge holes, did not amount to "good bread" in this modern age; though that too would change over the next decade.

POINT REYES

Back home, we reasoned, I would be free to make whatever I wanted. The market would determine my fate. I took their advice to heart and reluctantly returned to Northern California in 1994. Borrowing money to live on, we had severe culture shock that made us want to run right back to France. The feeling was short-lived, though, and we had work to do.

Liz and I knew of an oven builder residing in the hills above Tomales Bay north of San Francisco. Alan Scott lived in a large farmhouse on a ranch with a wood-fired oven out back. By this time, he had been building ovens for a few decades and was renowned for his simple, elegant design: a very efficient, clean-burning masonry oven.

West Marin County, along the coast of Bolinas and Tomales Bay, is filled with historic cattle ranches and organic and biodynamic small farms and vine-yards. This part of the country had a vibrant food culture with enough charms of the French countryside we so missed.

I contacted Alan, and he offered us room and board if we would help around the house and property. Eager to try his oven, I began baking bread a few days a week at the ranch. Alan was happy to see his oven in regular use. He insisted on grinding his own flour and often mixed a batch of his excellent Desem bread, a natural-leavened whole grain bread made from freshly ground wheat berries, to bake while the oven was hot. Alan's Desem on the lunch table told us that he'd been busy grinding grain and tending his leavens.

Alan didn't waste heat, using the oven for days as it cooled to cook pots of beans, dry vegeta-bles and herbs, and to make stocks of toasted grain muesli and granola.

Over a breakfast of whole grain buttered toast and steel-cut oats—his stalwart morning routine—we asked Alan's advice about how we might get a small bakery started closer to town. Straightaway, he offered to build us an oven and loan us the money to get going. His trust and generosity were immediate.

We moved from the ranch in Marshall to a house in Point Reyes on main street Route 1, across from Cowgirl Creamery, then still under construction. With Alan directing, friends and neighbors helped us build a wood-burning masonry oven next to our home. We were soon bartering fresh bread for wild salmon, abalone, oysters, ducks, eggs, fresh fruit, and garden vegetables. Liz made pastry, using the oven early before it was fired hot or after it had cooled sufficiently.

Continuing my focus on bread, I drew on the traditional bread-making discipline I had learned during my apprenticeship in the Berkshires and in France—while still searching for the loaf with an old soul.

In France, I had fallen in love with the sweet, creamy flavor of bread fermented with wild yeast leaven that contradicts the widespread perception of "sourdough." I wanted anything but sour bread. I wanted a deep auburn crust to shatter between the teeth, giving way to tender, pearlescent crumb. I wanted my baker's signature, the score made with a blade on top, to rise and fissure, and the crust to set with dangerous edges. Rustic forms from the forge of the oven would be the final expression of the process. To gain a following for these large, crusty loaves, I would make sure to bring bread that was still warm from the oven to the markets.

I began by doing things the way I had learned, but my present circumstances were different and required adjustments. I had no mixer. Kneading hundreds of pounds of dough daily by hand might have been an impossible task for a lone baker, but the wet dough was comparatively easy to develop by hand. I "kneaded" the dough in buckets by gently folding it at regular intervals. Following the wisdom of nineteenth-century French matrons and the centuries-old baking tradition of trough kneading, I let time and fermentation do the work.

During those early years in Point Reyes, the small bakery was a laboratory for three ingredients and a world of possibility: flour, water, and coarse gray salt from the Guérande in southwest France. I made most discoveries by exhaustive trial and error, over time gathering each lesson into a simple approach based on what I had learned. The approach was not rigidly scientific, but results were documented by concise shorthand notes and photos of the bread on days when something notable was achieved in crust or crumb. After years of baking in Point Reyes, I made the loaf I was after.

Our country loaf was distinct in a market already saturated by artisan bakers, and people soon took notice. The lab had become an atelier. Baking grew from three to five to seven days a week to make ends meet.

While I made local deliveries on foot in Point Reyes, Liz drove our '53 Chevy wagon packed with pastries and warm bread to the Berkeley farmers' market, where people had lined up in the lot an hour before.

After six years in the countryside, Liz and I moved our small business for a short time to Mill Valley, and then into San Francisco. We took over the lease of an all-but-retired corner cake bakery and in early 2002 opened our doors as Tartine.

COUNTRY BREAD IN THE CITY

Since 2002, Tartine, and our whole block of restaurants and shops, has become a hub of Mission life. We've maintained our tradition of "baking in real time." Our bakers pull hot croissants and quiches from the oven starting just before we open and into the early afternoon. The morning production occupies the deck oven until 2 P.M., and the bread is baked in the afternoon. The first loaves are out just before 5 P.M. and sold fresh for dinner. Production has remained on the same small scale since the first bakery in Point Reyes.

The new, urban setting necessitated the trade of our wood-fired masonry oven for a massive, gas-fired deck oven. Firing a gas oven never matches the satisfying ritual of burning wood but watching the fuel go up in smoke had come to weigh heavily on me. Real timber is too precious a resource to burn in ovens when an alternate fuel source is available. Nowadays in France and the rest of western Europe, most of the wood-fired ovens use pressed sawdust "logs" or scrap wood left over from construction or wood craft.

Any flavor imparted by the wood fire is imaginary. The inside walls of a wood-fired oven turn black from the soot when the fire begins to burn. When the temperature rises above 600°F, the soot begins to burn off. The walls are burned clean, and the baker sweeps and mops the hearth before loading bread. When I started baking years ago, many bakers in Northern California used eucalyptus wood to fire their ovens. It's cheap and burns especially dirty—but the oven still comes out clean. Thankfully, the bread gets no flavor from the wood burned.

Some who knew my bread from Point Reyes were skeptical of the switch from a wood-fired oven to a gas-fired deck oven. They worried that the bread would lose something special. I was not concerned. The key to making good bread is not the oven—any oven that can store and radiate heat, and trap steam, will work. The eventual nature of the crust is largely determined before the loaf is ever baked.

The baker's skill in managing fermentation, not the type of oven used, is what makes good bread. This fact makes *Tartine Bread* possible. I would not attempt a book with the home baker in mind if the results could never live up to the images. They can. And they will.

As always, it's in the bakers' hands.

CHAPTER 1

Basic Country Bread

THIS IS THE MOST BASIC RECIPE FOR THE BREAD I've been making since the beginning in Point Reyes. The approach and method form the foundational technique for all the other bread recipes presented here. This is the bread I miss eating when away on travels.

The process is simple and is accompanied by images illustrating the key steps. The thought, borne out by our test bakers, is that anyone can pick up this book and make a good loaf of bread using this chapter alone.

The basic recipe is followed by an in-depth explanation of the primary parts of the process, focusing on the practical knowledge that will enable you to expand on the basic recipe to make the variations and to tailor your baking to your specific needs. I recommend reviewing both the recipe for Basic Country Bread and the Basic Loaf in Depth section before making bread. Keep in mind that you'll need time and experience baking yourself to really understand how things work.

You'll find the tester profiles here as well. The excellent bread they made is as good as any I've eaten—ever. I trust their baking will inspire you in the same way that they inspired me.

For the Basic Country Bread and the other breads in this book, you will need the following kitchen tools: a digital scale for metric measures, a small scoop for flour, a thermometer, a wide bowl for mixing, a rubber spatula, a dough spatula, and a bench knife. At Tartine, we use a wide metal bowl to mix the ingredients with the least amount of mess. For baking the Basic Country Bread and other loaves, you will need a dutch oven combo cooker. Any other special equipment is noted in the recipe where it is required.

BASIC COUNTRY BREAD

Making bread with natural leaven can be divided into three basic stages. First you must develop a vigorous starter. Then you manage the wild yeasts and bacteria in the starter by maintaining a consistent routine, building to make a leaven to raise your dough. Finally you'll shape and bake the dough into a loaf of bread. The recipe for Basic Country Bread makes 2 loaves.

Making a Starter

Developing a starter begins with making a culture. A culture is created when flour and water are combined, and the microorganisms—wild yeasts and bacteria present in the flour, in the air, and on the baker's hands—begin to ferment spontaneously. After fermentation begins, the baker "feeds" the culture regularly to "train" it into a lively and predictable starter.

1) Mix 5 pounds of bread flour—half white and half whole wheat. You will use this 50/50 flour blend to feed your culture and develop your starter. All-purpose flour will work as well. Fill a small, clear bowl halfway with lukewarm water. Add a handful of the 50/50 flour blend to the water and mix with your hands to achieve the consistency of a thick batter with no lumps. Use a dough spatula to clean the clumps off your hands and tidy the inside of the bowl. Cover the bowl with a kitchen towel and place in a cool, shaded spot for 2 to 3 days.

2) After 2 to 3 days, check the culture to see if any bubbles have formed around the sides and on the surface. If the culture seems inactive, let it sit for another day or two.

By this time, a dark crust may have formed over the top of the mixture, which is typical. Pull the crust back and note the aroma and bubbles caused by fermentation. In this initial stage, when the culture smells strong like stinky cheese and tastes sharply acidic, it is very ripe. Now it is time to do the first feeding.

3) To feed the culture, discard about 80 percent of it. Replace the discarded portion with equal amounts of water and the 50/50 flour blend. Mix to combine just as you did in step 1. You have now begun training your culture into a starter.

Repeat the discarding and feeding process once every 24 hours at about the same time each day, preferably in the morning. Don't worry too much about the quantities of water and flour in these feedings—you want a thick batter. The important thing is that you feed the starter and pay attention to its behavior as it develops.

As the balance of yeast and bacteria is established, the volume of the starter will increase for several hours after feeding and then begin to collapse as the cycle winds down. Note how the aroma of the starter changes from stinky and sharply acidic to sweet and milky just after the feeding, when the starter is at the freshest or youngest stage in the cycle. "Fresh" and "young" are expressed and understood here in two ways: 1. the sweet stage of ripeness having been fed the normal 20 percent inoculation (2 to 4 hours) and 2. and/or many more hours (4 to 8) after having been fed using a very small inoculation (5 percent), yet still at the same sweet ripe stage. When the starter ferments predictably—rising and falling after feedings—you are ready to prepare a leaven and mix your first bread dough.

Keep in mind that training your starter is a forgiving process. Don't worry if you forget to feed it one day; just make sure to feed it the next. The only sure way to mess up a starter is to neglect it for a long period of time or subject it to extreme temperatures. Even then, a cycle of regular feedings will usually restore the vitality of your starter.

Making the Leaven and Mixing the Dough

When your starter is rising and falling in a predictable manner, you are now ready to make bread. When preparing to mix a dough, bread bakers use weight measurements. Measuring the flour, water, and salt by weight allows the baker to visualize bread recipes as parts, or ratios, of the whole. As you learn to make a variety of different bread recipes, you'll see how closely related they are. For ease of calculation, the bread recipes throughout the book use metric weights.

1) The night before you plan to mix the dough, discard all but 1 tablespoon of the mature starter. Feed the starter with 200 grams of warm (78°F) water and 200 grams of the 50/50 flour blend. Cover with a kitchen towel and let the starter rise overnight at a cool room temperature (65°F). This is your leaven.

By the morning, the leaven will be aerated by wild yeast activity, and the volume will have increased by about 20 percent. The most reliable indication that your leaven is ready is if it floats in water, a result of the carbon dioxide gas produced by wild yeast activity. To test the readiness of your leaven, drop a spoonful of it into a bowl of moderate room-temperature water. If it sinks, it is not ready to use and needs more time to ferment and ripen. You can expedite the fermentation by putting the leaven in a warm place and checking again after a half hour.

Your leaven should smell sweet in an overripe-fruit sort of way. I call this a young leaven, meaning it has not fermented to the point that it smells vinegary. If your leaven does smell vinegary in the morning, you have two options. You can mix the dough using this leaven, but with the expectation that your bread will taste more sour. Or you can discard half of the leaven and add 100 grams of warm water and 100 grams of the 50/50 flour blend. Doing this dilutes the acidity of the leaven and gives it fresh resources to ferment and ripen. Let the new mixture ferment until it passes the float test, about 2 hours.

2) Gather the ingredients listed on the table for mixing the dough. For convenience, put the 80°F water in a pitcher.

Bakers think in terms of ratios and express these ratios as percentages. The flour, no matter what quantity is used, is the constant 100 percent against which every other ingredient is measured and considered. Starting with this basic recipe and continuing for the rest of the book, the recipes are based on 1,000 grams (1 kilogram) of flour. This is designed to help you think like a baker. When you understand the principles of the basic ingredients and how they act in combination, you can adjust recipes to gain your own desired results.

The amount of water relative to the flour is called the hydration percentage. Dough made with 600 grams of water and 1,000 grams of flour is 60 percent hydration. In other words, the amount of water is 60 percent of the weight of the flour. The basic country dough here will be 75 percent hydration. The table below is the formula for the basic country dough in this chapter. Here we start with 75 percent hydration—making the dough easy to work with from the start. As you get comfortable with softer doughs, you can increase the percentage of hydration gradually to suit your taste.

INGREDIENT	QUANTITY	BAKER'S PERCENTAGE
Water (80°F)	700 grams plus 50 grams	75
Leaven	200 grams	20
Total Flour	1,000 grams (1 kilogram)	100
White Flour	900 grams	90
Whole Wheat Flour	100 grams	10
Salt	20 grams	2

3) Weigh 700 grams of the 80°F water and pour it into a large mixing bowl. Add the 200 grams leaven and stir it to disperse. (Be sure to save your leftover leaven—this is now your starter. If you plan to bake bread every few days, continue discarding a portion of the starter and feeding it daily, as instructed in step 3 on page 46. If you want to bake only intermittently, see page 71 about maintaining your starter.)

Add 1,000 grams flour—900 grams white and 100 grams whole wheat—to the water and mix thoroughly by hand until you do not see any bits of dry flour. Clean your hands and the sides of the bowl with a dough spatula. Let the dough rest for 25 to 40 minutes. Do not skip the resting period. Working with the nature of the dough, the resting period allows the protein and starch in the flour to absorb the water, swell, and then relax into a cohesive mass.

4) After the resting period, add the 20 grams salt and the 50 grams warm water to the dough. Incorporate the salt by squeezing the dough between your fingers. The dough will first break apart and then will re-form as you turn it in the bowl. Don't worry if the salt does not seem to dissolve right away. Fold the dough on top of itself as shown in the photos and transfer it to a small, clear container. At Tartine, we use a container made of a material with insulating properties, to maintain the warm temperature of the dough during this crucial development stage. If you have never made bread, it's instructive to be able to see the aeration of the dough as it develops. We like thick plastic because it is safe and easy to clean. A heavy glass bowl would also work well.

The dough has now begun its first rise, called the bulk fermentation or bulk rise. This crucial step should not be rushed, as its primary purpose is to develop flavor and strength in the dough. The bulk rise is highly temperature sensitive, and as a rule, warmer dough ferments faster. At Tartine, we try to maintain the dough at a constant temperature between 78° and 82°F to accomplish the full bulk fermentation in 3 to 4 hours.

One important consideration is that a small mass of fermenting dough will quickly equalize with the ambient room temperature. The speed of fermentation therefore greatly depends on the ambient temperature of your kitchen. However, there are many ways to create a microclimate for your dough. If your kitchen is cool—below 60°F—you can mix the dough with warmer water, 90°F for example, and keep the plastic container covered with a top made of a low-conductive material such as wood or thick, hard plastic. You can also use your oven as a makeshift proof box by putting a small pot of boiling water in the oven near the dough. This will raise the ambient temperature of the oven. Alternatively, if you use a baking stone in your oven, you can heat the oven briefly with

the stone inside (on a separate shelf from where your dough will be). When you turn the oven off, the heated stone will keep the oven warm.

If you want to leave for a few hours, a longer, cooler bulk fermentation might be desirable. Page 74 explains how the bread-making process can be tailored to fit your environment and schedule.

5) Using my technique, you'll notice that the dough is never kneaded on a work surface. The dough development that bakers usually achieve by kneading is accomplished here by giving the dough a series of "turns" in the bowl during the bulk fermentation. This process is cleaner than kneading outside the bowl and accomplishes the same degree of development with much less work.

To do a turn, dip one hand in water to prevent the dough from sticking to you and then grab the underside of the dough, stretch it up, and fold it back over the rest of the dough. Repeat this action two or three times so that all the dough gets evenly developed. This is considered one turn.

During the first 2 hours of the bulk fermentation, give the dough one turn every half hour. During the third hour, notice how the dough starts to get billowy, soft, and aerated with gas. At this later stage, you should turn the dough more gently to avoid pressing gas out of the dough.

Proper development during the bulk fermentation enables the wet dough to hold its shape as a loaf, and the baker must watch for signs of development and determine when the dough is ready. During the first hour of the bulk fermentation, the dough will feel dense and heavy. Watch how the surface becomes smooth

soon after you turn the dough. By the end of the third hour, the dough will feel aerated and softer. A well-developed dough is more cohesive and releases from the sides of the bowl when you do the turns. The ridges left by the turn will hold their shape for a few minutes. You will see a 20 to 30 percent increase in volume. More air bubbles will form along the sides of the container. These are all signs that the dough is ready to be divided and shaped into loaves.

If the dough seems to be developing slowly, extend the bulk fermentation time. Watch your dough and be flexible.

6) Use the dough spatula to pull all the dough out of the container onto an unfloured work surface. Lightly flour the surface of the dough and use a bench knife to cut the dough into two equal pieces (remember, this recipe makes enough bread for two loaves). As you cut the first piece, use the bench knife to flip it so that the floured side rests on the work surface. Do the same with the second piece of dough.

At this point you want to incorporate as little flour as possible into the dough. Fold the cut side of each piece of dough onto itself so that the flour on the surface of the dough is sealed on the outside of the loaf. The outer surface of the dough will become the crust, so you may use more flour on your hands to avoid sticking.

Using the bench knife and one hand, work each piece of dough into a round shape. Tension builds when the dough slightly anchors to the work surface while you rotate it. By the end of the shaping, the dough should have a taut, smooth outer surface. You want to develop a strong tension in as few movements as possible—use decisive yet gentle force while handling the dough. If the surface rips, you have gone too far in developing tension. Don't worry if it does rip—this is just an indication you should stop shaping and let the dough relax.

7) After this initial shaping, let both rounds of dough rest on the work surface for 20 to 30 minutes. This stage is called the bench rest. Make sure the dough is not exposed to drafts, which will cool it too much. A draft also can cause a dry skin to form on the top of the dough, compromising the final shaping. You may need to lightly flour the dough and cover it with a kitchen towel.

During the bench rest, each round will relax and spread into a thick pancake shape. The edge around the circumference should appear fat and rounded, not flat and tapered or "dripping" off the edge. If the edge is flat and the dough is spreading too much, these are indications that the dough did not develop enough tension during the bulk fermentation. To correct this, simply shape each round a second time—which is like giving the dough an extra turn in the container.

8) To form the final loaf shapes, lightly flour the top surface of the dough rounds. Slip the bench knife under each round to lift it off the work surface, taking care to maintain the round shape. Flip the round so that the floured side is now resting on the work surface. What was the underside is now facing up.

The final shaping involves performing a series of folds—taking care as always not to deflate the dough. The successive folding builds tension inside each loaf so that it holds its form and rises substantially when baked. Bakers call this dramatic rise "oven spring."

First, working with one round at a time, fold the third of the dough closest to you up and over the middle third of the round. Stretch out the dough horizontally to your right and fold this right third over the center. Stretch the dough to your left and fold this third over the previous fold. You are now starting to get a neat package.

Stretch out the third of the dough farthest from you and fold this flap toward you, over the previous folds, and anchor it in place with your fingers. Then grab the dough nearest to you and wrap it up and over, while rolling the whole package away from you so that the smooth underside of the loaf is now the top and all the seams are on the bottom.

Cup your hands around the dough and pull it toward you, rounding it against the work surface to tighten the tension and stretch the outer surface to close the seam. Let the shaped loaf rest for a minute. Repeat the folding with the remaining round.

9) In a small bowl, make a 50/50 mixture of rice flour and wheat flour. Line two baskets or medium bowls with clean kitchen towels and lightly flour the towels with the flour mixture. The patina of flour prevents the dough from sticking during the final rise. Using the bench knife, lift each shaped loaf off the work surface and transfer it to a basket or bowl so that the smooth side is down and the seam is centered and facing up. The loaves will now rise in preparation for baking.

At this point you have two options. The dough can rise at warm room temperature (75–80°F) for about 3 to 4 hours before baking. This is called the final rise, and at 2 hours, it will yield mild-flavored loaves.

If you don't want to bake right away, you can delay or "retard" the process by placing the dough, in the baskets or bowls, in the refrigerator for up to 12 hours. The cool environment slows, but does not stop, the fermentation. After 8 to 12 hours, the dough will develop more complex and mildly acidic flavors.

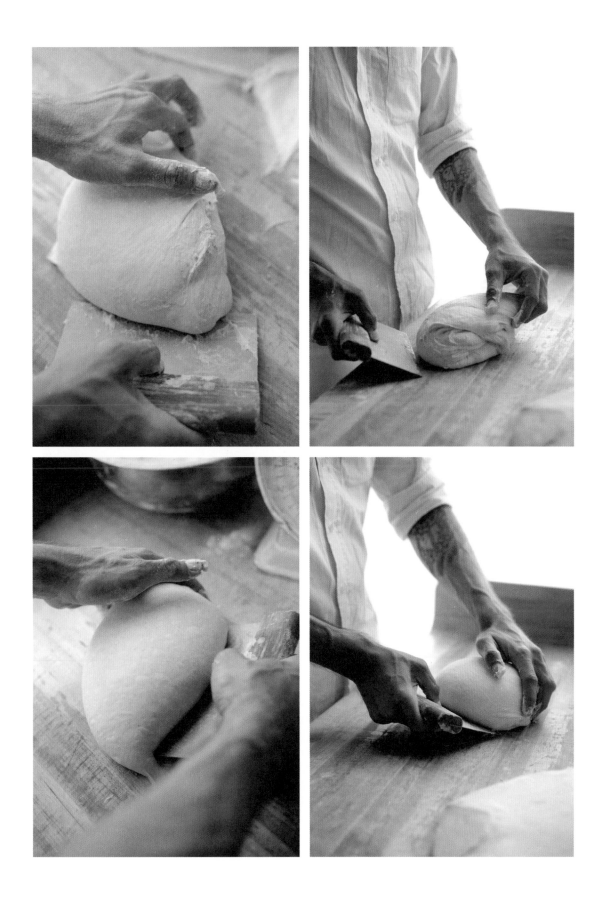

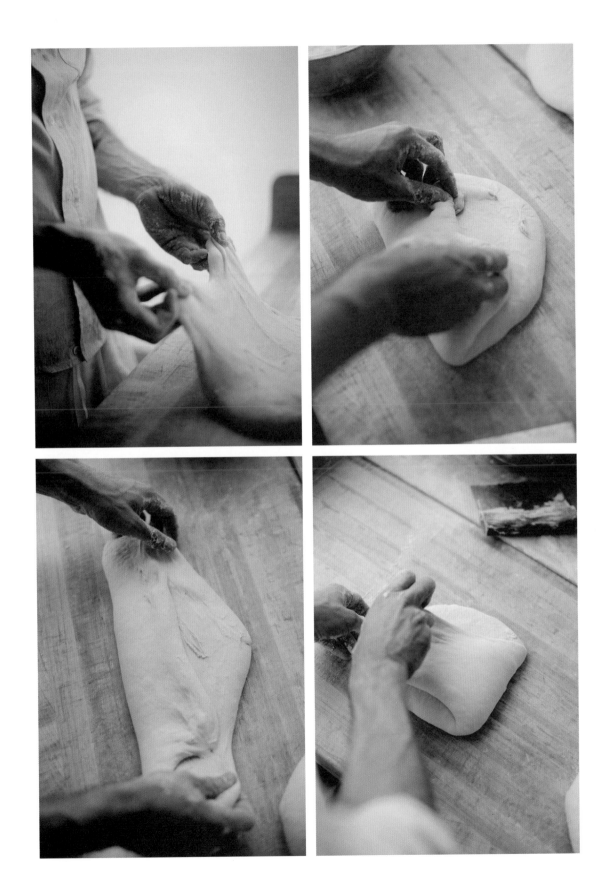

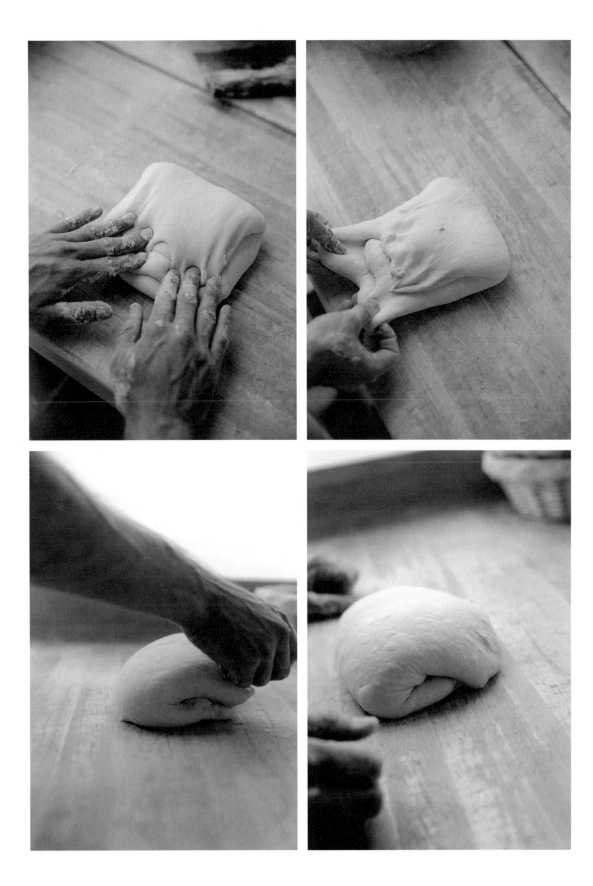

Baking the Loaves

1) About 20 minutes before you are ready to bake, place a dutch oven combo cooker (both pot and lid) in the oven and preheat the oven to 500°F. If the shaped dough is in the refrigerator, take one of the loaves out now. Leave the other loaf in the refrigerator until you are done baking the first one and have wiped clean and reheated the combo cooker and oven.

2) While the oven is preheating, gather your tools: heavy oven mitts, rice flour, and a double-edge razor blade to score the top of each loaf before it bakes. Razor blades can be tricky to use, so prepare a wooden splint to hold it. Split a wooden coffee stirrer halfway down its length, using the edge of a table. Then insert the blade onto the splint.

Bakers saturate their ovens with steam before loading the bread. The moist heat during the first 20 minutes of baking is essential to allow for the expansion of the loaves without forming a crust. All the characteristics that I strive for in a good loaf—burnished crackling crust, rich auburn color, open scores, and full volume— are enabled by this initial moist heat environment.

Home bakers are faced with the challenge of saturating with steam an oven designed to ventilate moisture. I have tried many methods for steaming in a conventional home oven, from wet towels to boiling pots of water, but no matter how much steam was created, it was impossible to trap enough moisture needed to achieve results at home similar to those from a professional bread-baking oven.

The sealed environment of a dutch oven solves this problem. It was a welcome discovery that, as with the wood fired ovens I had used for years, a dutch oven traps enough moisture from the loaf during the first few moments of baking to fill with steam. Using the dutch oven at home allows you to bake gaining the two main characteristics of a professional brick oven: a sealed moist chamber and strong radiant heat. The results using a dutch oven are indistinguishable from those using a professional baker's oven.

The photos here show my favorite dutch oven, a cast-iron combo cooker. One part is a shallow frying pan, and the other is a deep pan; each can act as a lid for the other. I like to bake bread on the shallow pan covered with the deep pan. The low walls make it easy to score the loaf prior to baking, and the deep pan used as a cover gives the loaf room to rise. Any dutch oven will work fine—just make sure you can cover the pan with a secure lid to seal.

3) Dust the surface of one of the loaves in the basket or bowl with rice flour. When the oven reaches 500°F, put on the kitchen mitts and carefully pull the heated shallow pan out of the oven and place it on top of the stove. Leave the other pan, or lid, in the oven. Please exercise extreme caution when handling the cooker. The pans are 500°F and will cause severe burns if your hands are not protected. Carefully inverting the basket or bowl, turn the dough into the hot pan. If the dough sticks to the towel, use more rice flour mixture the next time.

4) The loaves are cut or scored to help them fully expand in the oven. An unscored loaf will not rise to its potential and will often burst open along the sides. The angle, quantity, and pattern of the scores all affect how the loaf expands in the oven and determine the final appearance of the loaf. Experienced bakers use techniques that give them the effect they want, and types of scores can become signatures. Scoring is also used to distinguish different types of breads and to determine the aesthetic of the final loaf.

Make your scoring pattern on top of the loaf with the corner edge of the razor blade. For a round loaf, I suggest a simple square with four cuts. If you want the loaf to have pronounced "ears," make shallow cuts at a very low angle (almost horizontal) to the dough.

If your loaf is in the deep pan of the combo cooker or in a conventional dutch oven, take care not to burn your forearms on the edge of the hot pan while scoring the loaves.

5) Return the shallow pan holding the loaf to the oven and cover with the deep pan. You can invert this if the deep pan seems too heavy. If you do so, take care not to burn your forearms by touching the edges of the hot pan while scoring the loaves. Immediately reduce the oven temperature to 450°F. Bake the loaf for 20 minutes.

6) After 20 minutes, wearing the oven mitts, open the oven and carefully remove the top pan. A cloud of steam will be released. Notice that the color of the crust is pale and shiny. This is an indication of a well-steamed loaf. Continue to bake the bread until the crust is the color of deeply caramelized, 20 to 25 minutes. If you want a crackling crust that will stay crisp, it is important to bake your loaf out strong—until it reaches a burnished, golden brown color.

7) Wearing oven mitts, remove the pan from the oven and transfer the loaf to a rack to cool. If you don't have a rack, lean the loaf on its side so that air can circulate around the bottom. The loaf will feel light in the hand, which tells you that the right amount of water has been cooked out. When tapped on the bottom, the loaf will sound hollow.

To bake the second loaf, raise the oven temperature to 500°F. Wearing oven mitts, wipe out the cooker with a dry kitchen towel and reheat both the shallow pan and the deep pan for 10 minutes. Follow steps 3 through 7 for baking the second loaf. As each baked loaf cools, the crust contracts slightly. Listen for a faint crackling sound—the song of bread.

The Essential Ingredients

The most elemental bread is made from flour, water, and salt. This is the loaf of the Basic Country Bread recipe. Of these three ingredients, flour is the most important in determining the character of the final loaf. The flavor of the bread comes from the flour and the effect that fermentation and then baking have on it. Whole-wheat and rye flours ferment more actively than white sifted-wheat flours.

The freshness of the flour has a significant impact on the flavor of the final loaf. For those of us who don't mill our own flour, "fresh" flour means that it was milled a week or two before baking with it. I recommend using sustainably grown, freshly milled flour from as locally distributed a source as you are able to find. Excellent bread can be made by milling your own flour and using it to make bread as soon as it cools, but note that fermentation will be noticeably more active when freshly milled.

Most wheat flours labeled "all-purpose" will work for making bread. At Tartine, we performed a series of baking tests with three sample flours. One was a nationwide brand of bleached all-purpose flour bought from the corner mart; the bag was hidden on the shelf and looked as if it had been sitting there for months. The second was an organic "bread flour" with a good reputation, purchased from a natural foods store. The third was our own blend of flours milled by the miller I've worked with for fifteen years.

To our surprise, it was almost impossible to tell the resulting loaves apart by the outward appearance. We performed a blind taste test and immediately chose the bread made from our own flour out of the group. The flavor was absolutely distinct.

The loaf made from corner-mart flour had some unpleasant flavors that were not related to fermentation and were possibly a by-product of the flour processing or of some aroma that the flour had absorbed while sitting on the shelf. The loaf made with organic flour was good, but the crumb was tougher than I like. Through trial and error, I had long ago settled on a blend of wheat flours to achieve the tender crumb I want.

Since the beginning of my baking days, millers always want to show me lab statistics regarding their flours. Although knowing this information can help quantify your preferences, there is no substitute for making bread with the flour and tasting the results to learn if it suits your taste and your technique. Numbers don't always add up to the loaf you expect—baking "by the numbers" is best left to industrial operations.

Water that is good to drink is fine to use in bread. Temperature is the most important factor regarding water, as it's the most direct way to set the base temperature of your dough.

At Tartine, we use sea salt. Any salt is fine to use if it's good to eat. If using coarse sea salt, such as gros sel de Guérande, add it when mixing the dough in step 3 on page 52, as it will take some time to dissolve. Fine salt should be added after the dough has rested, as in step 4 of the same method.

The Starter

A baker's true skill lies in the way he or she manages fermentation. This is the soul of bread making.

Starter is a mixture of flour and water set to ferment. This fermentation happens naturally. After regular, successive feedings, bacteria that produce lactic and acetic acid along with wild yeasts establish themselves as fermenting agents in a symbiotic relationship. Sourdough starter cultures around the world are closely related, many of them having the same dominant strains of yeast and bacteria.

To begin, in my specific approach, there are two important things to consider regarding starter in relation to leaven:

1. A mature starter must be used to mix the leaven. The starter will be strongly ripe smelling and moderately acidic.

2. The leaven must be used to mix the dough when it is young and sweet smelling—long before it starts to smell anything like the starter.

When I traveled back to France to find Daniel Colin and Patrick LePort in 2008, I had not seen them for fifteen years. The talk almost immediately turned to bread and the intricacies of the leavens we were each using. I had brought photos of the bread I was making, and Daniel and Patrick wanted to know the feeding schedules and percentages I was working with at Tartine.

When I described the young, sweet-smelling liquid natural leaven, Patrick smiled and, reaching into a cool chamber, pulled out a small white bucket to show me. He said he had been experimenting for some time, but was not yet able to use this type of starter to leaven the bread to his liking. Incredibly, it was the same starter that I had been using for many years, starting in Point Reyes, and the same one I use now in San Francisco. The two starters must have been supporting the same microflora, as the aroma and flavor were identical. Indeed, after discussing our maintenance, we discovered we were on the same feeding schedule.

Wild yeasts are on the grain, on the baker's hands and, to a lesser extent, in the air. The bacteria, which need to be nourished, are living microorganisms that eat simple sugars and excrete lactic and acetic acids as waste. Wild yeasts eat different sugars and produce carbon dioxide during fermentation. The ratio of lactic acid to acetic acid produced is affected by the temperature of the environment in which the starter is maintained, the percentage of the seed amount (what you start with), and the frequency of the feedings. Refreshing a starter on a regular schedule with the same amount and blend of flour while storing the starter in a temperature-stable environment (ideally 65° to 75°F) will train it into a predictable and lively natural leaven.

Starters that are stored at higher ambient temperatures (not refrigerated) and are more liquid favor lactic acid production over acetic acid production. The overall acid load, or concentration of acid, in the final loaf is responsible for the sour flavor. Acid load begins when the fresh leaven is seeded with an already acidified portion of starter. At Tartine, we promote the flavor of the mild lactic acid over the vinegary acetic acid by controlling the production and importation of these acids during the feeding and fermentation stages. We always feed at moderate room temperatures using a small seed amount (less acid transfer), and we feed often—a few times per day depending on the season.

Strongly acidic bread occurs when a high percentage of acidic leaven is used in the dough and/or the rising times are overly long, either during the bulk fermentation or during the final rise.

Storing the starter under refrigeration regularly or for weeks at a time will promote bacteria and yeast that thrive at lower temperatures; favoring the production of acetic acid. To restore a less-sour flavor balance, after the starter is removed from the refrigerator, much of it should be discarded. The remainder, about 20 percent, is used to seed the next feeding to make a fresh starter. Discard about 80 percent of the refrigerated starter and add equal amounts of water and the 50/50 flour blend, following step 3 on page 46.

The role of the starter is to develop strength and acidity. In the subsequent leaven building, this strength, but not the acidity, is transferred to the larger mass of dough. The ripe, acidic starter conditions the gluten in a beneficial way by adding strength, but the amount is small enough that it does not add an intense acid flavor to the dough.

The Leaven

Floral, fresh, creamy, silky, sweet, milky—these are the qualities that you want to develop in the leaven and that will carry into your dough.

The leaven is made with the starter. The character of the leaven is transferred to the dough and ultimately to the final bread. The seeding of a large mass of dough by the leaven eventually transforms the entire dough into a larger version of leaven. If left to ferment beyond its prime leavening stage, the dough will become the starter again, completing the cycle.

The aroma of the leaven, as well as the dough, is the primary indicator that guides you through the stages of fermentation so that you know what is happening, regardless of temperature and time variables. Time and temperature are good places to start, but learning to read the "nose" of your leaven and dough at different stages will enable you to recall and repeat successful bakes and manage the process with skill.

If the leaven is overly ripe and vinegary when you mix the dough, the acid will overpower the other desirable flavors. You can still make bread with the dough, but quality will be compromised. Use less leaven to correct.

Half of an overly ripe leaven can always be discarded and fed with enough of the 50/50 flour blend and water to replenish it. The leaven will be ready to use when it reaches the sweet-smelling stage and passes the float test again (see step 1 on page 47)—in about 2 hours when held at a moderate room temperature of 76° to 78°F. Leavens mature at different rates depending on the ambient temperature at which they are maintained. Ideally, you want to use the leaven within an hour or two of when it's ready. Although the "young" leaven technique allows for a large window of time here.

If you are not able to control the ambient temperature in colder climates, use warmer water to feed the leaven with a higher seeding percentage of starter and give it one less feeding per day. In warmer climates, use a smaller seed percentage of starter and increase the daily feedings by one. In extreme heat, refrigerate the leaven to maintain a moderate temperature or use chilled water.

With experience, you will develop keen intuition in the rhythms of the baking cycle.

The Rest Period

The dough rests in the bowl just after the initial mixing. This period, named the autolyse (AUTO-leese) by esteemed French bread expert Professor Raymond Calvel, is now in common use.

While the dough is left to rest, glutens swell and form chains that become the gas-trapping structure of the dough. Autolyse improves the effectiveness of the time spent mixing (or turning by hand) while shortening the time needed to actively develop the dough. Calvel confirmed the notion of improved mixing by letting the dough accomplish much of the work passively. If you are short on time, even a 15-minute rest is better than none and increases the efficiency of the turns you are about to do.

Calvel quantified the autolyse and explored other beneficial actions that occur during this rest period, such as the conditioning of protease, an enzyme in the flour that is activated with hydration and works on the gluten to increase extensibility. Extensibility is the ability of the dough to stretch easily while not pulling back, or bucking. It's an important quality that is essential to achieve good volume in your bread.

The Bulk Fermentation

The first rising of the dough is called the bulk fermentation or the bulk rise. This is when the strength, flavor, and structure of the dough are set. The French call this phase *le pointage*, referencing the importance of judging "the point" in the process when the development is optimal.

Flour is made up of starch and protein. When it is hydrated with water, the starch and proteins absorb the water and swell. The proteins form connected chains that constitute the structure of the dough, which is developed by stretching and folding the dough as you give it turns during the bulk fermentation. The resulting tiny air pockets form the base cell structure of the crumb. They fill with gas during the bulk rise and expand during baking to create an open-textured crumb. The low-acid/high-hydration approach in this book necessitates a lengthy bulk fermentation during which the structure of the dough is developed by turning the dough in its container. With each turn, the strength of the dough increases exponentially. Turns should be more vigorous at the start of the bulk fermentation and gentle toward the end so as not to deflate any trapped gas that is leavening the dough.

The bulk fermentation for the basic country dough is accomplished in 3 to 4 hours if the dough is maintained at a temperature of 78° to 82°F. The timing can be altered to suit your needs. If, for example, your environment is 65° to 70°F and your dough cools down, the rise will take a few hours longer. Once you are able to anticipate the effects of temperature changes on rising time, you can make this work for you. On days when I have to work the bread shift alone, I mix the dough 1° or 2°F cooler by using cooler water; this varies depending on the ambient temperature and the temperature of the flour. Doing this adds 1½ hours of bulk fermentation, so I can bake for the day, pack up orders, and clean baskets and cloths before I need to divide and shape the next day's dough.

Making natural leavened bread is forgiving and versatile. You will always use your leaven at relatively the same stage of ripeness, but the bulk fermentation time and the final rising time can be lengthened considerably to spread the process over two days. There are many ways to arrange this. One example is to accomplish the bulk rise during the day and the final rise overnight. Another is to achieve the bulk rise overnight and the final rise during the day so that you can bake in the afternoon before dinner.

If the dough is mixed using cooler water, at 65°F, it will need 8 to 12 hours of bulk fermentation, rather than 3 to 4 hours, as long as it's kept at 55° to 65°F. You can mix this cool dough in the evening before retiring. The key is to arrange your schedule to achieve convenience without compromise.

The bulk rising time can be shortened by mixing the dough with water that is a couple of degrees warmer, but it's best not to sacrifice more than an hour of bulk rise time.

If you let the bulk fermentation go too long, the final rise will be sluggish as the food that fuels the fermentation has been exhausted. The glutens in the dough also begin degrading after a certain point due to increasing acidity, which results in a tighter, more uniform crumb. The volume of the final loaf will be smaller, and the flavor more acidic. When the dough is baked, the crust will color faster due to residual sugars on the surface of the dough that caramelize too quickly, and the scores on the surface will not open well to form the decorative crust. Conversely, if the bulk fermentation is cut short, the dough will not be properly aerated. Lacking strength, the pre-shaped rounds will run on the tabletop during the bench rest. The baked color will be dull, and again, the scores will not open well—if at all.

When the bulk fermentation is well timed, the divided and shaped loaves will show a structure unto themselves. When baked, the scores will open elegantly, an expression of both the force within the loaf and the hands that shaped it.

The Shaping and the Bench Rest

When you are dividing your dough into two pieces for shaping, you can assess how it feels and decide how to proceed with the rest of the process. "Should I give the dough a long bench rest to develop more strength, or should I shape the dough twice to give more tension?" You can make immediate adjustments by allowing for a longer or shorter bench rest to ensure you get the results you want. If your dough cools down too quickly after you divide it, or if it seems heavy and not sufficiently aerated, warm up the room and give the dough more time on the bench before shaping. Generally speaking, if the dough is divided too early, you need more time and maybe an additional shaping with a 15-minute rest in between. Take your time—it will only make the bread better.

One evening at Tartine, I divided my country dough too early even after a long bulk rise. The marine layer had rolled into our neighborhood and caught me off guard. The doors and windows were open, and the temperature dropped 20°F in 10 minutes. The fermentation slowed to a crawl. To compensate, I had to give the dough a very long bench rest. Breaking for dinner, I ate next door at Delfina and came back later to shape the loaves. By allowing time to correct the situation, I ended up with flavorful and beautiful loaves.

Divide your loaves too late, and you'll need to shape the dough swiftly and gently, keeping as much air intact as possible. In this case, you'll want to bake sooner rather than later—adjusted from whatever you've developed as your normal baking schedule.

The intial shaping of the dough sets structure for the final shape. With highly hydrated doughs, the final shape is crucial for developing the tension or force needed for the loaf to maintain its form throughout the long final rise. Proper final shaping is also essential to achieve the dramatic arced "ears" that bloom forming a decorative crust when your scores expand and open.

Although the overall volume of a well-shaped loaf and a poorly shaped one may be the same, the scores will not open on the poorly shaped loaf with the same expression as the scores on a well-shaped one. Structural shaping is deceptively simple and takes practice to master, but with the skill comes the freedom to craft any bread you imagine.

We achieve the necessary tension by using a series of decisive folds, each one adding structure at points within the loaf. Common practice is to press air out of the dough and roll it tight. This knocks precious gas, an essential flavor component formed during the long rise, out of the dough and toughens the crumb. Once you get the hang of structural shaping, it's a pleasure with ample reward.

The Final Rise

The final rising time is variable. At warm proofing temperatures around 80°F, loaves will be ready to bake in 3 to 4 hours. If you don't retard the final rising, your bread will have little to no perceptible sour flavor, and the flavor of the wheat will be more up-front. You still gain the benefits of sourdough: your bread will stay fresh longer, and it will have a more complex savor.

Retarding, or slowing, the final rise by cooling the loaves and holding them in the refrigerator enables you to control two key things: when you bake your bread, and the intensity of the flavors. During a longer final rise, flavors gained from fermentation build to an optimal intensity and then become increasingly sour.

So you have a wide range to work with. You can make delicately flavored bread that no one would think to call sourdough, or you can make substantially stronger-flavored bread to your taste.

The Bake

This is the final act in producing your bread. I began baking with a gas-fired hearth deck oven during my apprenticeship with Richard Bourdon. This lasted a couple years until I went to work in France using "indirect" wood-fired ovens. When I finally opened my first bakery, I opted for a "direct" wood-fired masonry oven. I wanted to learn to bake in the most primitive way possible, and this was it. Plus, I couldn't even afford a dough mixer, much less a professional deck oven.

In a directly fired or "black" oven, the fire is built inside the domed chamber where the bread will be baked, and it burns for hours to saturate the masonry mass with stored heat. Wood is added intermittently, and the fire is shifted around the floor of the oven so that all parts of the baking chamber are evenly heated. An indirectly fired or "white" oven has a firebox outside the baking chamber where the fuel is burned, and the flame from the fire is directed into the chamber. The inside chamber of a black oven turns black from the fire's smoke and soot. When the interior gets hot enough, it burns off clean. White ovens have vented chambers to pull off the smoke and soot, so the chamber does not turn black.

At Tartine, we bake at an initially high oven temperature and then turn the oven off. The idea is to use the modern oven as I used the wood-fired ovens. A massive masonry oven, heated directly, stores that heat and then radiates the heat to bake bread with a falling temperature once the direct heat source is off. Radiant heat, in combination with conductive heat, is thorough and penetrating, well suited for baking highly hydrated doughs.

When we built the bakery in Point Reyes, we turned to Alan Scott, the most renowned builder of wood-fired masonry ovens in the United States. A key aspect of his brilliant design was the closed baking chamber. When the chamber was filled with loaves and the small door on the front of the oven shut, the oven was completely sealed. As bread began to bake in the steam-filled chamber, the fermentation activity quickly and dramatically increased. This rapid production of gas, along with the quickly expanding steam pushing against the walls of the gluten structure, caused oven spring, the initial expansion of volume in the baking loaf. The moist baking environment allowed for more expansion before the crust formed, resulting in a superior volume and a light, open crumb in the final loaves. The starch on the surface of the loaves was moistened and gelatinized during baking to give a slight sheen to the crust. With the combo cooker, you are able to achieve this effect at home, one loaf at a time.

Expensive modern deck ovens are equipped with steam injectors that humidify the chamber before and during loading. Steam injectors are a necessity, as deck ovens require a lot of steam just before loading with bread to saturate the chamber with moisture and during the first 10 to 15 minutes of baking until the deck is full of bread, which then generates its own steam.

Baking your bread in a cast-iron combo cooker gives you the same results you'd get with a professional deck oven by creating a completely sealed, radiant-heat environment. The loaf itself generates the perfect amount of steam until you remove the cooker lid to allow the formation of the crust to finish the bake. The cooker's sealed steam-saturated chamber gives considerably better results in oven spring and score development than baking a loaf on a baking stone placed in a home oven. During our tests using baking stones, when the oven was fully saturated and closed, we watched steam pouring out of seams all around. It's not possible to replicate the same environment in a standard home oven without creating a sealed oven inside the oven. That is what the combo cooker does.

Once the oven spring has been achieved and the crust is starting to set, you vent the steam by removing the cooker lid to allow the formation of the crust and its gradual but thorough caramelization. When the crust is well colored and the loaf sounds hollow when tapped on the bottom, the bread is done. The interior temperature of the loaf will read 212°F. The loaf will have a lightness in the hand, indicating that the right amount of water has been cooked out of it.

Bread that cools slowly will keep fresh longer. Stack the loaves together on edge and let them cool for 2 to 4 hours. This is not necessary, though. It's a great pleasure to pass a hot loaf from the oven to a bread lover. I prefer to eat fresh bread very fresh. Otherwise, I fry it in a pan with olive oil or butter, toast it, or make one of the recipes in Chapter 4 using day-old bread. In any case, it is always eaten. Frying a slice cut from a loaf still warm from baking will yield an exquisite delicacy—crisp, fried edges with a custardy interior.

Jeffrey Steingarten, author of *The Man Who Ate Everything*, once asked me, "What good is making great bread if nobody gets to eat it but you and your friends?" The answer comes easy once you bake your first loaf.

TEST BAKERS

Training an apprentice to bake bread is one thing, but teaching someone how to do it in print is quite another. I knew that the most important aspect of this book would be the effectiveness of the recipe for Basic Country Bread, so Eric and I asked friends to help us translate this Tartine loaf into their respective home-baking scenarios. Eric set up a password-protected blog and posted the photos and text as I planned the material to be published.

Enlisting a group of a dozen committed test bakers, we supplied them with dutch oven combo cookers and posted the first round of photos and instructions. Initially I wrote very simple instructions, hoping to encourage the testers to approach the process with a close eye on the images with the freedom to learn from their experience. Soon photos, personal accounts, and questions started pouring in. A vibrant discourse ensued as many plunged into the project with focused enthusiasm.

It was clear that I had work to do on the basic recipe, but I never expected such consistently impressive results. Many testers made exceptional bread, judged by professional standards—it was virtually indistinguishable from our own Tartine bread. Their bread gave us no reason to take into consideration that they were making it at home, with no experience and without professional equipment. Granted, the testers who prevailed were dedicated and genuinely interested in building a leaven to make great bread.

A few testers started modifying the recipe to suit their schedules. Eric and I, along with Nate Yanko, my lead bread baker at Tartine, and Lori Oyamada—the freshest face to join the bread shift—were making bread for the daily production while continuing to assemble and test other recipes for the book. There was no time to maintain the blog properly, and our testers went rogue. When we caught up with them months later, they were doing their own thing—with impressive results.

When we told friends about the book project, our testers' experiences were what resonated the strongest: The grad student who had never baked before made better bread than most commercial bakeries. The former chef and avid home baker got results he had practically given up on. The first-time restaurant owner decided that he wanted to make the bread for his cafe instead of buying it.

Our testers prove that great bread is possible, no matter how little time or experience you have. They innovated along the way, and we all became better bakers for it.

Marie:

Every other Friday at Tartine, we are treated to the music of a fine accordion player and her trio. Marie has a warm smile and an engaging personality, and volunteered to be a tester before we finished telling her about the idea. She was a full-time grad student and a working musician with no baking experience whatsoever.

Marie started her "bread adventure" right away and posted detailed accounts of her experience. She described her early efforts with the starter in personal terms, as if she were getting to know someone. She admitted it was "awkward" at first. She carried her starter on a weeklong trip to Brooklyn, playing shows nightly, and baked her first loaf two days after she returned to the West Coast.

She also came up with her own simple and effective baking aid. She made a chart on index cards with five columns: (1) baking stages, (2) estimated time each stage takes (from basic recipe), (3) planned time, (4) actual time, and (5) temperature of the room/oven for each stage. The chart was so handy that she used it every time she baked. She was able to work out her baking schedule ahead of time, and plan the rest of her day deciding whether she wanted to mix in the morning or the afternoon. Once she had the stages and their approximate timing on the chart, she could plug in different times to figure out how best to fit baking into her schedule. "It allowed me to get errands done, go for a run, and edit papers—my day ended up being so much more productive than it would've been if I hadn't baked bread."

Marie had already baked eight times when we went to see her at home. Though her bread was coming out beautifully, she noted that the actual times no longer matched the estimated times. Luckily she had saved all the cards, with everything in detail. Reviewing the cards, we noticed a remarkable progression. At first she was very strict about controlling the ambient room temperature, and the entire process kept very close to the estimated schedule. After the fourth baking session, her room temperature fluctuated (a normal occurrence in the Bay Area), and the actual times were off by a few hours.

Far from viewing this as a fault, we saw it as an indication that she was developing a real baker's intuition. Rather than baking by the numbers, she was responding to the dough. The first few baking sessions taught her what to look for. Then, when cool room temperatures threw the starter and then the bulk fermentation off, she waited, increasing her rising times, instead of rushing the process.

Though she now leaves her starter behind when she travels, Marie continues to bake. She uses her note cards but with an extra element of control: she controls the ambient temperature during the bulk fermentation to shorten or extend the timing based on her schedule of activities for the day. She loves eating and sharing her loaves, but what she most looks forward to is the faint crackle of the hot crust as it cools—the "song" of the bread.

Mark:

If Marie showed that this method works well for the complete novice, Mark would be proof that it offered something useful for more experienced bakers. He had worked in a bakery when he was in his early twenties and since then had read most books on the subject. A meticulous, self-effacing "science geek" with a quick sense of humor, he pressed us for details to bolster his already strong intuition. We sent him a combo cooker and insisted he start by doing exactly what he saw in the pictures.

Mark had been baking bread at home for years—with a long, passionate detour into doughnuts—and was skeptical about my claim that he could make Tartine bread in his home oven. His early loaves were stunning, and the basic country recipe is better for his pointed and insightful questions.

We went to his home in Sebastopol to bake with him. A stickler for details, he stayed close to the original method. He controlled the ambient temperature during the bulk rise by using the oven as a proofing chamber (see page 52). Instead of using a pot of hot water, he turns on the oven for a few minutes every half hour to heat his baking stone. (He claims he hasn't yet forgotten to turn it off.) He uses half of the dough for pizza and the other half for bread, which he bakes the same day.

"First, I can't believe that I have bread like this in my home made by my own hands. One bite, and I said, 'This tastes like real bread.' I was always stymied in my attempt to make bread with the texture and crust that is possible from a proper bread oven. I felt that there was a ceiling on the quality possible from something baked traditionally at home and was accepting that belief (with a great deal of therapy I might add).

"What you have helped me with is a better understanding of and skills with my starter. Since it is literally the heart, soul, and life of these breads, all of the rest is decoration until a lively dough can be created. While I had read about the cast-iron method before, your dough comes out much better using it than on any previous dough I made and baked that way. The magic, then, is clearly in the method."

With that, the conversation turned back to doughnuts.

Dave:

We met Dave in the water, a surfer and artist who had supported himself for years as a bartender, a few months before he and his wife were set to open a small café a block from our home break—Ocean Beach. He had recently leased an abandoned, barely equipped restaurant space. Dave poured the last of his savings into the café and hired a small staff with the understanding that he had no cash flow and could pay them based only on what the restaurant made day to day.

Dave was doing most of the remodel and repair work himself. He had just finished a beautiful mosaic made of Northern California driftwood. Earlier in the month, he had learned to mill wood so he could panel the entire wall with salvaged, worn redwood fence boards. Despite his do-it-yourself philosophy, he knew his limits in the kitchen. He couldn't be the chef of his restaurant, but he still wanted to play a part in creating the food, and he mentioned wanting to make the bread himself.

I thought it was a lot for him to take on at the time, as they had a baby due around the time they were scheduled to open the place. But I understood his motivation and devised a simple method that would enable Dave to make good bread with little time and no experience.

I brought him five pounds of flour and explained how to make a starter. I directed him to the tester blog and told him to call me with any questions. A few months passed without a word, until one day we got a call at the bakery: "We've been open for three months, and people are going nuts over the bread. When are you guys coming in?"

The next time we saw Dave a couple of months later, he had a baby daughter; the restaurant was full and had a crowd waiting outside for open seats; and his bread was on every table. His loaves looked like driftwood, reminding me of the rustic bread of "the awesome baker" in Bordeaux years ago, and the inside crumb was spongy and moist. It had the balanced acidity you get only from a long fermentation with a young starter. Though his bread had many of the characteristics we strive for, it was a unique loaf and beautifully matched the aesthetic of his small café.

Eric stayed that night to watch Dave make bread. Over the previous few months, he had radically departed from my original method. He didn't do it intentionally—he really thought he was doing things close to the way that I had shown him—but he admitted he had read the recipe only once.

We could see that the limitations of his schedule and equipment had necessitated a completely different approach. He doesn't have a large oven (forget free-form hearth loaves), a large refrigerator (forget retarding), or even a mixer. What he does have is a few free hours in the evening after the dinner service and, under a six-burner range, a single convection oven with a broken door from which he needed to pull forty loaves a day.

Although Dave didn't have the know-how to conceive a baking schedule from the outset, he had adapted to his circumstances. He mixed his leaven between lunch and dinner service at around 5 P.M. He then mixed the dough a few hours later, when the dinner shift was winding down, developing the 78 percent hydration dough with turns every fifteen minutes. The bulk fermentation lasted for barely an hour before he divided and shaped the dough. After a thirty-minute bench rest—during which he washed dishes and finished cleaning—he shaped the loaves and put them in metal loaf pans brushed with olive oil. After slashing the loaves with a razor—"What, you guys really do this right before you bake?"—he let them sit out and rise overnight. The bread was baked at 7 A.M. the next morning, often before or after a quick surf session.

Had he consulted me before, I might have advised a different system. But the proof was in the results: Dave's bread is excellent and fits perfectly within his constraints. But why does it work?

Dave can't bake free-form loaves because he doesn't have a big enough oven. So he uses pans. This was a lucky coincidence, because the pans are the key to the success of his fermentation schedule. Because he can't make bread until after the dinner service, his dough undergoes bulk fermentation for only an hour. It still feels lifeless when he divides and shapes. This would spell disaster for a free-form hearth loaf, which relies on the tension developed during the bulk fermentation to hold its shape during the long final rise.

But Dave doesn't have to worry about the lack of tension because the loaf pans support the dough all the way through to the bake. He can't do a long bulk fermentation (as it is, he finishes shaping around midnight), so he makes up for it with a long rise in the pans at room temperature (about 65°F). If he did have the time to give the dough a "proper" bulk fermentation according to the basic recipe, his bread would be ready to bake in the middle of the night. He would need to retard the fermentation, but he does not have the refrigerator space to retard the loaves in his small café.

As it is, Dave is able to squeeze the active working time into a narrow window. Then he lets the long rise overnight do the rest of the work, so that his bread is ready to bake when he wakes up the next morning. His bread rises overnight at room temperature in the restaurant. The young starter here is key. If he didn't use it, his bread would be overwhelmingly sour and dense.

There is a buzz in the neighborhood about Dave's bread—a development that genuinely surprises him. He recounts with good humor the conversations with excited customers who ask him how long he has been baking bread. "I want to tell them I really don't know what I'm doing."

The bread is a small but essential part of Dave's broader vision for the business. Despite the fifteen-hour days, he is happy with how things are going: "It's the first time I have not had to compromise myself to do something. I'm doing work that's thoroughly in line with my ethics. There is no part of this restaurant that I'm not proud of." He looks over to his wife and young daughter. "It's not just the ethics, though; the reason it's working so well for us is that it's in line with who we are. The fact that it's situated in our neighborhood among people we know. The restaurant, the bread . . . they're just an extension of ourselves and an honest portrayal of who we want to be."

Having little free time means prioritizing the things he wants to do most. "My dream will be realized when I can surf every day that it's good, spend time with my family, and then put in a solid day of work among friends."

VARIATIONS ON BASIC COUNTRY BREAD

I worked alone for a decade, chopping wood daily, firing the oven, and mixing doughs by hand. Early on, it became clear that I could not maintain the quality I wanted mixing multiple doughs with each one fermenting at different paces while I handled the demands of a one-man bakeshop. If I wanted to maintain consistency, I had to simplify things. So I mixed one large dough per day, added ingredients to flavor, and employed different shapes to offer my regular customers a range of breads to choose from.

All of these breads use the basic country dough. The procedure for adding the ingredients to the dough is the same for all variations—during the bulk fermentation, generally after the first turn. Don't worry if the dough feels as if it's breaking apart. It will come back together after a few minutes' rest.

The amounts for the additions in each variation are enough for one recipe of basic country dough, which yields two loaves. If you want to make two different variations with one dough mix, divide the dough in half after the first turn and add half of the additions to each piece of dough. Of course, add more or less to suit your taste.

Olive

At Tartine, we like a mix of green olives and oil-cured black olives. For a spell, I insisted on using only green *lucques* olives. This was my favorite version of our olive bread, but it took hours for us to pit the olives by hand for the quantity of bread we produced. Pitting olives would certainly be worth the effort on a small scale. Taste different olive varieties and use the ones you like the most. Another variation I first made in Mill Valley incorporates toasted walnuts or hazelnuts along with the olives and herbs. There are a lot of flavors at once with this one, but eaten with a round of piquant goat cheese; fresh, ripe figs or persimmons; and our local greens, the olive-nut bread makes a fine meal.

Makes 2 loaves

3 cups pitted olives, coarsely chopped

2 cups walnuts or hazelnuts, toasted and coarsely chopped (optional)

2 teaspoons dried *herbes de Provence*

Grated zest of 1 lemon

1 recipe Basic Country Bread dough (page 45)

In a bowl, stir together the olives, nuts (if using), *herbes de Provence*, and lemon zest. After giving the dough a first turn in step 5 (see page 54), add the olive mixture to the dough and moisten with a little water. Use your hands to cut and incorporate the ingredients into the dough. Complete the bulk fermentation as directed.

Sesame

Deeply toasted sesame seeds lend an unexpected depth of savor to the bread. After you incorporate the seeds into the dough, the sesame aroma gets stronger as it mixes with the aromas of natural fermentation. The flavor mellows after the dough is baked. This bread can be used interchangeably with the Basic Country Bread and is a standout in places you might not expect: grilled cheese sandwiches, peanut butter and jelly sandwiches, steak and eggs on toast, and Pan con Tomate (page 199).

Makes 2 loaves

1 cup unhulled sesame seeds
1 recipe Basic Country Bread dough (page 45)

Preheat the oven to 400°F. Spread the sesame seeds evenly on a rimmed baking sheet. Bake the seeds for 10 minutes. Remove from the oven and redistribute the seeds—those near the outer rim will be darker than those in the middle. Continue to bake the seeds until well toasted, 10 to 15 minutes. Let cool for 20 minutes.

After giving the dough a first turn in step 5 (see page 54), add the cooled seeds to the dough and moisten with a little water. Use your hands to cut and squeeze the seeds into the dough. Complete the bulk fermentation as directed.

Walnut

Walnut bread should have nuts in every bite. It is expensive bread to make using good, organic nuts, and worth doing well. As for the sesame seed variation, the walnuts are toasted to intensify their flavor. Tannins in the walnuts streak the dough purple. If you like, also incorporate walnut oil. A decadent addition of 2 tablespoons of fine walnut oil (or more or less to taste) provides an added layer of walnut flavor.

Makes 2 loaves

3 cups walnuts

1 recipe Basic Country Bread dough (page 45)

Preheat the oven to 425°F. Spread the walnuts evenly on a rimmed baking sheet. Bake the nuts for about 15 minutes, stirring every 5 minutes so they toast evenly. To test for doneness, break open a walnut. The inside should have a light caramel color; the outside should be a shade darker. Let cool for 20 minutes. Break the nuts in half, or coarsely chop them if you want smaller pieces.

After giving the dough a second turn in step 5 (see page 54), add the walnuts to the dough and moisten with water. Use your hands to cut and squeeze the nuts into the dough. Complete the bulk fermentation as directed.

Polenta

Any grain—as long as it is cooked or soaked in hot water and then cooled—can be added to the Basic Country Bread dough. Using a coarse polenta soaker I first experimented with at Bourdon's in the Berkshires, this bread was an early favorite at the Berkeley Farmers' Market. Along with the Bolinas People's store, Toby's Feed Barn, Tomales Bay Foods, and Manka's Inverness Lodge, the Berkeley Farmers' Market sustained our small business for many years.

Steep coarse-ground polenta in boiling water before mixing it into the dough. The polenta adds a custardlike texture to the crumb, and golden corn oil adds more depth to the corn flavor. The toasted pumpkin seeds and fresh rosemary complement the nature of this bread well.

1 cup pumpkin seeds

1 cup polenta

2 cups boiling water

3 tablespoons unrefined, unfiltered corn oil

1 tablespoon chopped fresh rosemary

1 recipe Basic Country Bread dough (page 45)

Preheat the oven to 400°F. Spread the pumpkin seeds evenly on a rimmed baking sheet. Bake the seeds until they start to pop and turn from light green to brown, about 10 minutes, stirring them once after 5 minutes. Let cool for 20 minutes.

In a bowl, stir together the polenta and boiling water and set aside for 30 minutes or until cool. Stir the corn oil, rosemary, and pumpkin seeds into the polenta.

After giving the dough a second turn in step 5 (page 54), add the polenta mixture to the dough and moisten with a little water. Use your hands to cut and squeeze the ingredients into the dough. Complete the bulk fermentation as directed.

Pizza

By the time the final shaping is finished on the bread shift, the bread bakers are the last ones left at the bakery. On occasion, we pinch some dough and bring it to the apartment upstairs to make pizza for dinner. We're fortunate to have an old gas oven with a shelf broiler and broken thermostat. With the heating element cranked to broil and a terra-cotta tile positioned right above it, the oven turns out a blistery pie in about 3 minutes. Our current pizza revival, with all the attitude, manifestos, and "secrets" (the flour! the water! the oven!), is amusing. Just start with good bread dough and a very hot baking stone, and you will end up with a great pizza.

Nettle

You'll need a pizza peel and a baking stone or ceramic tile at least 12 inches square.

Makes 1 pizza

400 grams Basic Country Bread dough (page 45)

Cornmeal for dusting

All-purpose flour for dusting

cont'd

6 cups fresh nettle leaves

½ cup heavy cream

Red pepper flakes

Salt

2 ounces mozzarella cheese, cut into ½-inch cubes

2 ounces fontina cheese, cut into ½-inch cubes

Divide the dough as directed in step 6 on page 56, making sure that one piece weighs 400 grams. Shape each piece and let one round rest on the work surface for 30 minutes.

Meanwhile, position a rack in the middle of the oven and remove the other racks. Place the baking stone on the rack. Preheat the oven at its highest setting—about 500°F. Allow 15 minutes to thoroughly heat the stone.

When the oven is hot, dust a pizza peel with cornmeal. This helps keep the dough from sticking, and it eases the transfer of the dough from the peel to the stone. Dust the dough round with flour and transfer it to the peel, placing it flour-side down.

Dust the dough with a little more flour. Press the dough round ½ inch from the edge to create a rim. Lift up the dough and place the center onto the back of one of your hands. Stretch the dough using the back of your other hand so that it spreads from the middle. Rotate the dough around on your hand and let gravity help stretch it evenly. When the dough is sufficiently stretched, lay it on the peel. If the dough ripped while you were shaping it, press the tear back together. The diameter should be smaller than the stone but can vary depending on how thick or thin you want your pizza to be. Place the dough on the peel.

To make the topping, use tongs when handling nettles, as they will sting. In a bowl, toss the nettles with the cream and a pinch each of red pepper flakes and salt. Distribute the cheeses across the dough and mound the nettles on top. They will cook down quite a bit during the baking, so you can use many more nettles than you think.

Shake the peel to loosen the dough and make sure it slides easily. If it's stuck to the peel, use a spatula to lift it up and add more cornmeal under the dough. Open the oven door and place the far edge of the peel against the far side of the baking stone. Shake the peel and pull it out of the oven to slide the pizza onto the stone.

Bake the pizza for 4 to 8 minutes, depending on how hot your oven gets. Check the bottom of the pizza for char marks—an indication that the dough is baked through. When the pizza is done, slide the peel under it and remove from the oven. Place the pizza on a cutting board and cut into wedges to serve.

Margherita Pizza

Pizza Margherita is the classic Neopolitan pizza with scant-but-perfectly-balanced toppings. Baked blistering hot, traditionally in a wood-fired oven, the round of dough is sauced with a spoonful of tomato sauce. Torn pieces of fresh mozzarella are arranged on top, and the disk is peeled into a 900°F oven with a fire burning inside.

Cooked in under 2 minutes, the outside corona colors with charred blisters while the interior remains pliable. The Margherita is finished with freshly picked basil strewn over the bubbling sauce and cheese. Drip chili oil over the top for added heat, or good extra-virgin olive oil to add a rich note. Such perfect simplicity has become the iconic image of pizza across the world.

Here we use our home oven blasted on the broil setting to delicious effect. Our neighbor, and pizza obsessive, Jeff Krupman has modified a portable Weber home grill into a wood-burning pizza oven affectionately dubbed "the FrankenWeber."

When he's on the block, we prefer to use his rig.

Potato Focaccia

I first tasted this potato flatbread many years ago at Sullivan St. Bakery, then in Soho, hot from the oven and powerfully delicious. Trying to achieve something similar, I made this version after I got home. The potatoes are salted and drained, and the water that's pressed out is replaced with flavorful olive oil, which gives the baked potato topping a satisfying richness.

This is one of my favorite recipes from our days selling at the Berkeley Farmers' Market where I could always trade focaccia for a slice of Cheeseboard pizza. We often make a version of this flatbread for family meal at the bakery, topping it with whatever we have on hand: Concord grapes and fromage blanc; sweet peas and summer squash; corn and Padrón peppers.

You can use fresh dough as you would for pizza or a piece of dough that you've retarded overnight in the refrigerator. At the bakery, we pull a loaf from the rack that has fermented overnight, stretch it out, add the toppings, and bake.

Makes 1 focaccia

1 recipe Basic Country Bread dough (page 45)

3 pounds waxy potatoes such as Yukon gold

1½ teaspoons salt

Freshly ground pepper

½ cup olive oil

Leaves from 1 bunch fresh thyme

3 ounces pecorino cheese

If using fresh dough, shape it as directed in step 6 on page 56. Let rest on the work surface for 30 minutes. If using dough from the refrigerator, let it sit at room temperature for 30 minutes to warm up.

Using a mandoline, cut the potatoes into thin, translucent slices. Place in a colander and toss with the salt. Let stand for 20 minutes to release the liquid. Press or squeeze out the remaining liquid from the potatoes until they stop dripping. In a large bowl, toss together the potato slices, pepper to taste, olive oil, and half of the thyme leaves.

cont'd

Preheat the oven to 500°F. Brush a rimmed baking sheet with olive oil. Transfer the dough to the pan and stretch it to the edges. Don't force the dough if it tightens before you can spread it. Let it rest for a few minutes and continue stretching, taking care not to press all the gas out of the dough.

Distribute the potatoes over the surface of the dough. Bake for 15 minutes, then check the focaccia and rotate the pan to bake evenly. Continue baking until the focaccia is golden brown and the potatoes are crisp, about 20 minutes. Remove the focaccia to a cutting board. Shave or grate the pecorino over the top and garnish with the remaining thyme. Cut the focaccia and serve warm. Or let cool on a rack and then cut.

CHAPTER 2

Semolina and Whole-Wheat Breads

USING VARIETIES OF WHEAT THAT ARE LESS COMMONLY BAKED into bread, such as semolina, or varying the amount of whole-grain wheat will give your bread a different character from the Basic Country Bread while maintaining its essential qualities. Much of the basic recipe and method are the same.

SEMOLINA BREAD

The heart of the durum wheat berry, semolina is golden yellow and higher in protein than common wheat bread flour. Durum semolina is what gives pasta its characteristic yellow color. In southern Italy, finely ground semolina was most often cheaper than white sifted wheat flour and was used to make the daily bread of Sicilians, called *pane rimacinato*.

Traditionally, the bread was homemade, raised with natural leaven, and baked in a wood-fired oven. It was eaten warm or grilled with fresh ricotta, marjoram, anchovies, and olive oil. We fry a slice of the bread in olive oil and cut

it into batons to prepare a baker's snack of sheep's milk ricotta, walnut *Anchoïade* (page 187), and Calabrian chili paste, enjoyed with fresh figs and local honey from San Francisco's Mission District.

The higher protein content of semolina flour calls for more water in the mixing process to achieve a dough that feels similar to the basic country dough. A blend of semolina flour and regular wheat bread flour is used in an 70/30 ratio. While the semolina bread has a notably golden-colored crumb, the flavor is only slightly different from that of normal wheat bread. The additional flavoring of crushed toasted fennel, poppy, and sesame seeds complements the nature of the grain: as always, adjust the amounts to suit your taste.

Makes 2 loaves

INGREDIENTS	QUANTITY	BAKER'S PERCENTAGE
Leaven	200 grams	20
Water (80°F)	750 grams plus 50 grams	80
Semolina Flour	700 grams	70
All-purpose or Bread Flour	300 grams	30
Fennel Seeds	75 grams	7.5
Sesame Seeds	75 grams	7.5
Salt	20 grams	2
Mixed Seeds for Coating*	200 grams	

* Use a mixture of fennel, poppy, and sesame seeds, untoasted.

Prepare the leaven as directed in step 1 of the Basic Country Bread recipe (see page 45). When the leaven passes the float test, you are ready to mix the semolina dough.

Pour the 750 grams warm water into a large mixing bowl. Add the leaven and stir it to disperse. Add the semolina flour and the all-purpose flour. Using your hands, mix thoroughly until no bits of dry flour remain. Let the dough rest in the bowl for 25 to 40 minutes.

While the dough is resting, toast the fennel seeds and sesame seeds in a skillet over medium-high heat for about 5 minutes. Transfer to a small bowl to cool. Coarsely grind the toasted seeds in a mortar with a pestle or pulse in a spice grinder. Add poppy seeds to seed mixture.

After the resting period, add the salt and the 50 grams warm water to the dough. Incorporate the salt by squeezing the dough between your fingers. The dough will first break apart and then will re-form as you turn it in the bowl. Don't worry if the salt does not seem to dissolve right away. Transfer the dough to a clear container as directed in step 4 on page 52 and begin the bulk fermentation. Follow the instructions for turning the dough in step 5 on page 54. After giving the dough a second turn, add the ground fennel and sesame seeds to the dough and moisten with a little water. Use your hands to cut and squeeze the seeds into the dough. Complete the bulk fermentation as directed.

Follow steps 6 through 8 on pages 56 to 58 for the initial shaping, bench rest, and final shaping. After completing the final shaping, roll the top of each loaf in the mixed seeds. Transfer each loaf to baskets or bowls for the final rise, seeded-side down, as directed in step 9 on page 58. Bake each loaf, following steps 1 through 7 on pages 65 to 68.

VARIATION ON SEMOLINA BREAD

Golden Raisin, Fennel Seed, and Orange Zest

This dried fruit variation gives the loaf a sweeter flavor profile. Golden raisins and fennel seed are a classic combination. I enjoy this bread for breakfast, toasted and spread with butter and marmalade.

Makes 2 loaves

3 cups golden raisins

1½ tablespoons fennels seeds, toasted and crushed

1 teaspoon coriander seeds, toasted and crushed

1 recipe Semolina Bread (page 110)

Grated zest of 1 Valencia orange

Put the raisins in a bowl and add warm water to cover. Soak the raisins for 30 minutes. Drain and return to the bowl. Add the fennel and coriander seeds and orange zest.

After giving the dough a second turn in step 5 on page 54, add the raisin mixture to the dough and moisten with a little water. Use your hands to cut and squeeze the mixture into the dough. Complete the bulk fermentation, shaping and baking as directed.

WHOLE WHEAT: COMPLET AND INTEGRAL

Richard Bourdon introduced me to the artisan-style whole grain loaf. Like many of us whose mothers made lunch meat sandwiches on honey-baked wheat loaves, I grew up thinking that whole-wheat bread was a sweet, soft loaf resembling brown Wonder bread. To this day, I can't resist a bologna, cheese, and mayo sandwich on this bread. But Richard's bread was different—a free-form loaf with a moist crumb and a substantial, burnished brown crust.

Working in France with Daniel Colin and Patrick LePort, I found their signature breads included whole-grain hearth breads with similar characteristics to Richard's and these further informed the way I approached whole-grain baking. Both bakers made two versions of brown bread. The *complet* used a blend of white and whole-grain flours and produced a light wheat bread. The second, called *integral*, was made from 100-percent whole-grain wheat flour and had a darker, denser crumb with a more pronounced whole-wheat flavor. These are the loaves we lived on, along with pâté and flagons of rosé.

Whether *complet* or *integral*, dough with a high percentage of whole-wheat flour requires higher hydration than white bread, as the bran present in the whole-wheat flour absorbs more water. It is difficult to get the same open texture in a whole-wheat loaf. The bran particles puncture the developed gluten walls, which prevents the dough from holding as much gas and achieving the same volume as white flour does. I suggest starting with a *complet* dough, which has a lighter texture than the *integral*, and then adjusting the blend based on your preferences. The holy grail of a whole grain hearth bread with an open crumb like the basic country loaf is one that can be achieved—even as a fleeting anomaly wholly dependent on the seasonal qualities of the grain used. It's absolutely worth the trouble to get there.

At Tartine, we make our whole wheat with the same leaven we use for the Basic Country Bread. Some bakers insist on maintaining a second starter that is 100-percent whole grain for their dark bread, but for us it's not worth the trouble. Whole grain, after all, contains 100 percent of the "white" flour. If you wish to convert your leaven to whole grain, feed your starter a couple of times with all whole-wheat flour before making bread and you've got it. Note that the fermentation will be more active, so keep everything a bit cooler and/or feed with a reduced percentage of seed starter (about 5 percent less to start) to accommodate.

WHOLE-WHEAT BREAD

Since the whole-wheat flour absorbs more water than white, the dough benefits from a longer resting period after the initial mix. The rest for the basic country dough is 25 to 40 minutes; 40 minutes to an hour is good for whole wheat. Some bakers favor an overnight rest for whole grain—a technique worth exploring as long as you wait to add the leaven until you begin to give the dough turns.

Whole-wheat flour ferments more actively than white flour, so this dough uses slightly cooler water to slow down the fermentation. You can also adjust the percentage of leaven from 20 percent to 15 percent, but remember that a complete bulk fermentation is still essential to achieve proper tension in the dough before shaping.

Makes 2 loaves

INGREDIENT	QUANTITY	BAKER'S PERCENTAGE
Leaven	200 grams	20
Water (75°F)	800 grams	80
Whole-wheat Flour	700 grams	70
All-purpose Flour	300 grams	30
Salt	20 grams	2

Prepare the leaven as directed in step 1 of the Basic Country Bread recipe (see page 45). When the leaven passes the float test, you are ready to mix the whole-wheat dough.

Pour the warm water into a large mixing bowl. Add the leaven and stir to disperse. Add the whole-wheat flour and the all-purpose flour. Using your hands, mix thoroughly until no bits of dry flour remain. Let the dough rest in the bowl for 40 to 60 minutes.

Follow steps 5 through 9 on pages 54 to 58 for finishing the dough and steps 1 through 7 on pages 65 to 68 for baking the loaves.

Flax and Sunflower

This was another bread we first made at Bourdon's—a classic combination found in German whole-grain baking. I first tasted the combination in some corn chips and was instantly hooked. The flax seeds add a moist, supple quality to the crumb, and the bread keeps exceptionally well. After the loaf is shaped, it is rolled in sunflower seeds, which toast while the bread bakes.

Makes 2 loaves

2 cups flax seeds

4 cups boiling water

2 cups sunflower seeds

1 recipe Whole-Wheat Bread dough (page 114)

Before you mix the dough, put the flax seeds in a bowl and pour the boiling water over them. Let cool. The seeds will become gooey.

Preheat the oven to 400°F. Spread 1 cup of the sunflower seeds evenly on a rimmed baking sheet. Bake the seeds for 10 minutes. Remove from the oven and redistribute the seeds—those near the outer rim will be darker than those in the middle. Continue to bake the seeds until well toasted, about 5 minutes. Let cool for 15 minutes.

After giving the dough a second turn, as in step 5 on page 54, add the flax seed mixture and toasted sunflower seeds to the dough and moisten with a little water. Use your hands to cut and squeeze the seeds into the dough. Resume the bulk fermentation as directed. Follow steps 6 through 8 on pages 56 to 58 for the initial shaping, bench rest, and final shaping.

After completing the final shaping, put the remaining 1 cup sunflower seeds on a plate or tray. Roll the top of each loaf in the seeds. If the seeds do not stick, moisten the surface of the dough by rolling it over a wet towel. Transfer each loaf to baskets or bowls for the final rise as directed in step 9 on page 58. Bake each loaf, following steps 1 through 7 on pages 65 to 68.

Raisin and Coriander

I learned of the combination of raisins and freshly ground coriander seeds again from Bourdon, who held that coriander aided in digestion. At Berkshire Mountain Bakery, the "childrens," as Richard called his kids, often ate a whole warm loaf after school with butter. Currants may be used in place of the raisins. This bread is another sleeper hit when used to make grilled cheese sandwiches.

Makes 2 loaves

3 cups raisins

1 tablespoon coriander seeds

1 recipe Whole-Wheat Bread dough (page 114)

Put the raisins in a bowl and add warm water to cover. Soak the raisins for 30 minutes. Drain and return to the bowl.

Toast the coriander seeds in a small skillet over medium-high heat for about 5 minutes. Grind the coriander seeds in a mortar using a pestle or in a spice grinder. Just before mixing the whole-wheat dough, add the coriander to the raisins and stir to combine.

After giving the dough a second turn in step 5 on page 54, add the raisin mixture to the dough and moisten with a little water. Use your hands to cut and squeeze the raisins into the dough. Complete the bulk fermentation as directed.

Follow steps 6 through 9 on pages 56 to 58 for finishing the dough and steps 1 through 7 on pages 65 to 68 for baking the loaves.

Pain au Gruyère

One of my favorite whole-wheat breads we make at Tartine is inspired by the *pain au Gruyère* I first tasted at the bakery of Fernand Onfroy on the Rue de Saintonge in Paris. It's made by folding coarsely grated Gruyère cheese and freshly ground pepper into the dough at the end stage of mixing. The rectangular loaf is baked in a small cedar veneer box shaped like a bread pan, called a *panibois*, lined with parchment paper. Cheese melts out of the scores on top and caramelizes with the crust. The toasty aged Gruyère is a choice complement to the whole grain.

Makes 2 loaves

1 recipe Whole-Wheat Bread dough (page 114)

10 ounces cave aged Gruyère cheese, grated

Olive oil for brushing

Mix the whole-wheat dough as directed. After the flour is incorporated, add the grated cheese and mix thoroughly with your hands. Let the dough rest in the bowl for 40 to 60 minutes.

Follow steps 5 through 8 on pages 54 to 58 for finishing the dough. In step 8, shape the dough as directed. Brush two loaf pans with olive oil. Transfer the dough to the pans and let the dough rise for 2 to 3 hours before baking. Bake each loaf, following steps 1 through 7 on pages 65 to 68.

COUNTRY RYE

Rye flour has a distinct sweet grain flavor that develops when the dough is fermented with natural leaven. For some rye breads, such as traditional German ryes, an intensely sour flavor is preferred and is achieved by a long fermentation.

For the country rye loaves here, I use just enough rye flour to impart a distinct rye flavor and sweetness, while keeping sourness to a minimum. The whole-rye flour adds a slight gray cast and distinct tenderness to the crumb.

When using rye in combination with wheat flour, you can vary the portion of rye to suit your taste: as you increase the percentage of rye flour to wheat, the loaves will become more dense due to the lack of gluten in rye.

Use a medium-fine grind of whole-rye flour as opposed to a coarse pumpernickel rye, which will yield a very different result.

Makes 2 loaves

INGREDIENTS	QUANTITY	BAKER'S PERCENTAGE
Leaven	200 grams	20
Water (75°F)	800 grams	80
Whole-rye Flour (medium-fine)	170 grams	17
White Bread Flour	830 grams	83
Salt	20 grams	2

Prepare the leaven as directed in step 1 of the Basic Country Bread recipe (page 45). When the leaven passes the float test, you are ready to mix the dough.

Pour the warm water into a large mixing bowl. Add the leaven and stir to disperse. Add the rye flour and bread flour. Using your hands, mix thoroughly until no bits of dry flour remain. Let the dough rest in the bowl for 40 to 60 minutes.

Add the salt, and follow steps 5 through 9 on pages 54 to 58 for finishing the dough and steps 1 through 7 on pages 65 to 68 for baking the loaves.

CHAPTER 3

Baguettes and Enriched Breads

MAKING BREAD WITH NATURAL LEAVEN WAS THE RULE FOR French bakers up until a century ago. Before the introduction of baker's yeast as we know it today, bakers in the eighteenth and nineteenth centuries used brewer's yeast, a by-product of beer production, to lighten their loaves in combination with the natural leaven. In the latter part of the nineteenth century, baker's yeast was developed and bakers started to employ it. At first, bakers adopted the innovation cautiously. They mixed flour and water together with a small amount of yeast and let it rise for a few hours, just as they had been doing to make their natural leaven.

This prefermented batterlike leaven came to be known as a "poolish" (often attributed to Polish origin) and was used in combination with natural leaven. In these early days of yeast, even when the poolish was used alone to leaven, the bulk rise was lengthy, and final rise remained long and slow. The results were outstanding: the measured addition of commercial yeast to the dough made bread that was lighter than ever, and the proper use of natural leaven with long bulk rising times ensured that the bread had good flavor and exceptional keeping qualities. The overlap lasted a few decades. Raymond Calvel, a French baker who came of age in the early twentieth century (and became known as a renowned and somewhat idiosyncratic authority on French bread), referred to these decades as "the golden age of French bread." Natural leaven and commercial yeast were used in combination or exclusive and apart. Either way, bakers at the time understood and respected the tradition of gentle mixing and long, slow rising times at all stages to develop flavor and preserve the integrity of the craft.

The golden age was short-lived. Natural leavens require more work to maintain consistently in a large-scale bakery, and bakers abandoned the age-old practice in favor of the more convenient commercial yeast. As bakers added more yeast to their dough, they found they could inflate their dough quickly and omit the time-consuming bulk fermentation. This made their bakery production more efficient, but the quality of the bread was radically degraded. Bakers were aerating the dough instead of fermenting it, sacrificing flavor and altering the very nature of French bread—the soul of the bread had gone from it.

Bread that was once revered around the world now gained the reputation for staling within hours. Consumers balked. Although bread was still considered the staple of the French diet, historians note that bread consumption in France sharply declined after the 1940s. As bakers adopted yeast, they stopped teaching their apprentices how to bake with natural leaven, and the collective knowledge of how to use it was almost lost.

Since the demise of the golden age, dogma and superstition have kept the use of yeast and natural leaven mostly apart. Proponents split into distinctly opposing camps. For the bakers who held on to tradition, yeast became the enemy. Blame for the decline of the staff of life fell heavy on the tiny microbe. I knew of a French baker who turned a class of schoolchildren away from touring his boulangerie because he thought that yeast, hitching a ride on the unsuspecting children, might invade his bakeshop. His concerns were unfounded since the acidified environment of a natural leaven is not amenable to commercial yeast, posing little danger of contamination.

The artisan bread revival that took hold in the United States in the late 1980s had started in France a decade earlier. Many bakeries proudly announced that their bread was made without yeast. Naturally leavened bread, *au levain naturel*, was reclaiming its eminence from the century before. Some bakers, especially in Paris and also in a handful of other cities, were rediscovering the *levain de pâte* method, which harmoniously combined natural leaven and yeast to make a highly regarded style of bread.

At Tartine, I use the poolish as a yeasted liquid leaven in combination with our natural leaven in doughs when I want to achieve a lighter texture, a less pronounced acidity, and a thinner crust. I mix the poolish separate from the dough and use the amount that yields the results I want. The bulk fermentation and final rising times remain substantial and can be varied to suit the needs of the day.

BAGUETTES

Just as the country loaf was a vision worked toward for years, my ideal baguette existed long before it was made by me. I'm sure it has been consistently made somewhere since the birth of the French baguette in the early twentieth century, but I had not found it. This baguette might have been easiest to find in the early 1900s, when commercial yeast was proliferating, and bakers were using it judiciously.

I was confident I could bring this early baguette to our table at Tartine by using natural leaven in combination with commercial yeast. I first made a baguette using the basic country dough. The bread was a delicious, fiercely crusty version of the country loaf stretched into a baguette shape. Though worth making, it was not the baguette I was aiming for. I wanted a more subtle flavor than that of the country loaf and a thin, crisp crust.

After a few months of testing, I got the baguette I wanted by doubling the young leaven percentages, adding a large portion of poolish, changing the blend of flours, and extending the final rise. I prepared the poolish in the manner of our leaven and tried different percentages. The poolish contributes flavor in the same way that the natural leaven does, but without the bacterial fermentation, so there is none of the sour flavor from acetic and lactic acids. Poolish also increases the extensibility of the dough, helping to form an open, irregular crumb and a thin, crisp crust.

From the first test, I knew that I would not retard the rising overnight, as it yielded a thicker crust and stronger flavor than I wanted. When I used the same ratio of 20 percent leaven as in the basic country dough but baked the baguettes the same day, the results were good. Yet the flavor gained from the leaven was too subtle—almost bland—so I increased the amount. Even though I wanted to bake the baguettes the same day, I had to mix the baguette dough using cooler water (75°F) than for the basic country dough, as the addition of poolish and much larger percentage of natural leaven increased the fermentation activity.

Since the baguette dough would not be retarded overnight, the fermentation would not be lengthy enough to tenderize the gluten. Thus, I changed our regular mixture of mostly bread flour, adding a large portion of lower-gluten all-purpose flour. I also tried 5 to 10 percent white spelt flour (as a portion of the 100 percent flour) in some test versions, with excellent results. Spelt flour adds an extreme extensibility, as the gluten in spelt flour has a different character than that in all-purpose or bread flour. Ultimately, I settled on the mostly all-purpose blend for this recipe.

After the usual 3 to 4 hours of bulk fermentation, the dough is divided and shaped. The dough is soft and sticky, so I use a modified version of the technique for shaping the basic country dough. The shaped baguette dough is allowed to rise for up to 3 hours before baking.

The right balance of poolish, the increased amount of young leaven, and the softer flour blend—after many months of testing—yielded a baguette for the ages. Baked to a deep golden tone, this baguette has the toasty aroma of freshly popped corn.

Since a long baguette won't fit in a combo cooker, I recommend you bake the baguettes on a rectangular baking stone and saturate the oven with steam before loading, continuing for the first 10 to 15 minutes of baking (see page 134). Depending on the size of your baking stone, you may need to adjust the length of the loaves so that they fit on the stone. In addition to a pizza peel, you will want to have a hand peel for moving the shaped dough onto the pizza peel. A narrow rectangle of wood or a rigid cardboard flap from a box will work. For scoring the bread, have ready a double-edged razor blade in a splint holder (see step 2, page 65).

Makes 2 or 3 baguettes

POOLISH

200 grams all-purpose flour

200 grams water (75°F)

3 grams active dry yeast

LEAVEN

1 tablespoon mature starter (see page 45)

220 grams all-purpose flour

220 grams water (80°F)

Rice flour for dusting

BAGUETTES

INGREDIENTS	QUANTITY	BAKER'S PERCENTAGE
Leaven	400 grams	40
Water (74° to 76°F)	500 grams	50
Poolish	400 grams	40
All-purpose Flour	650 grams	65
Bread Flour	350 grams	35
Salt	24 grams	2

To make the poolish, in a bowl, mix the flour, water, and yeast. Let stand for 3 to 4 hours at a warm room temperature (75° to 80°F) or overnight in the refrigerator.

To make the leaven, place the mature starter in a bowl. Feed with the flour and the water, following step 1 on page 47.

The poolish and the leaven are ready when they pass the float test. Drop a small amount of the poolish and the leaven into water. If either sinks, it is not ready to use and needs more time to ferment.

To mix the baguette dough, measure the 400 grams of leaven and set aside the remainder to refresh and maintain as your starter. Pour the warm water into a large mixing bowl. Add the poolish and the leaven and stir to disperse. Add the all-purpose flour and the bread flour. Using your hands, mix thoroughly until no bits of dry flour remain. The baguette dough initially will feel a little stiffer than the basic country dough, but it will soften during bulk fermentation. Let the dough rest for 25 to 40 minutes.

Follow step 4 on page 52 to transfer the dough to a clear container and begin the bulk fermentation at a temperature of about 75°F. Turn the dough about every 40 minutes as instructed in step 5 on page 54; add the salt with the first turn.

When the bulk fermentation is complete, follow step 6 on page 56 to divide the dough into two or three pieces, depending on the size of your baking stone. Shape each piece into a rectangle with rounded corners. Let rest on the work surface for 30 minutes.

Drape a large kitchen towel over a baking sheet or cutting board and dust with rice flour.

Working with one dough rectangle at a time, fold the third of the dough closest to you up and over the middle third. Holding the ends of the dough, stretch it horizontally so that it doubles in width. Fold the third of the dough farthest from you over the middle of the elongated rectangle as if closing the flap of an envelope. Press on this flap to develop tension in the dough. Using your palms and fingers together, roll the dough toward you; with each successive roll, press with the outer edge of your palms and fingers to further develop tension in the dough. You should end up with a cylinder of dough shaped like a French rolling pin. Place both palms on the dough cylinder and roll it back and forth, stretching the dough to elongate the shape and taper the ends, while keeping in mind the size of your baking stone.

Shaping baguette dough is difficult because much more handling is required than for other shapes. With practice and persistence, this part of the process will become second nature.

Place the loaves on the floured towel seam-side up and separate them with folds in the towel. Bring the sides of the towel over the loaves to support the outer edges. Let rise at warm room temperature (70° to 75°F) for 2½ to 3 hours.

Place the baking stone on the middle rack of the oven and preheat the oven to 500°F. When using a baking stone, the trick is to saturate the oven with steam when you start baking. The best way to get as much steam as possible into a home

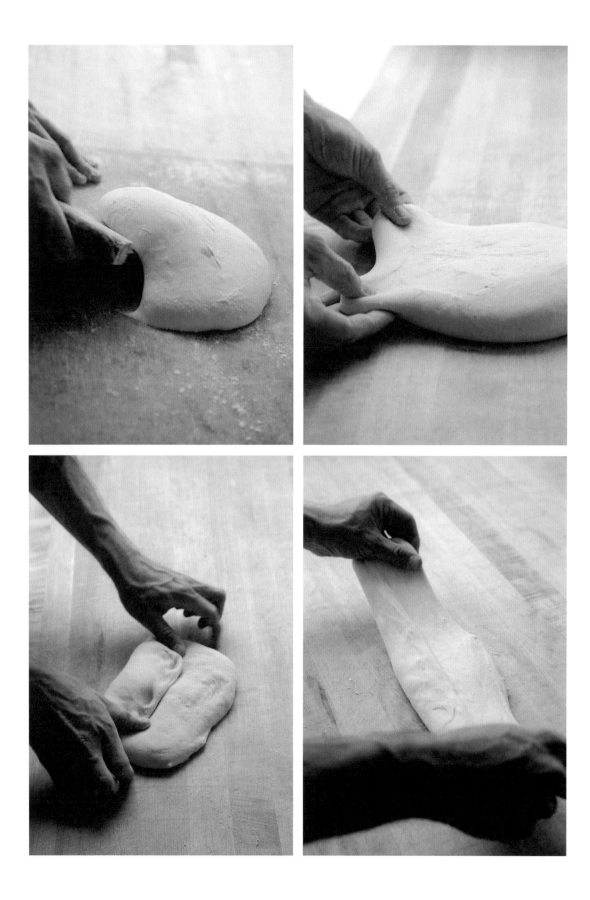

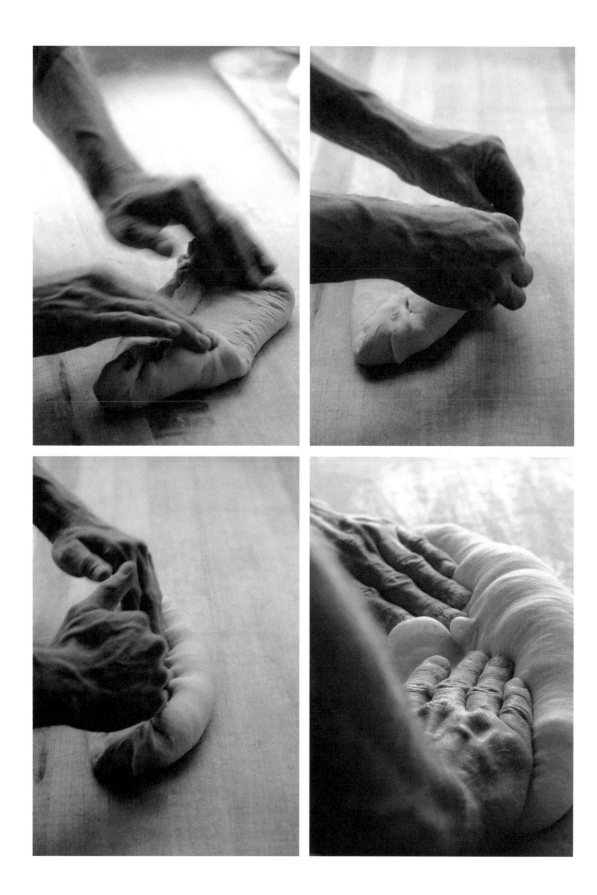

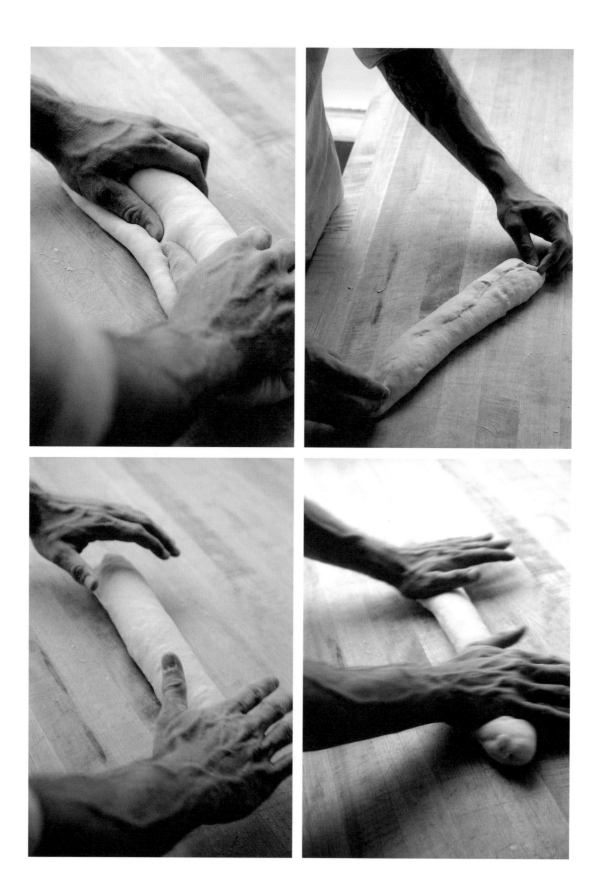

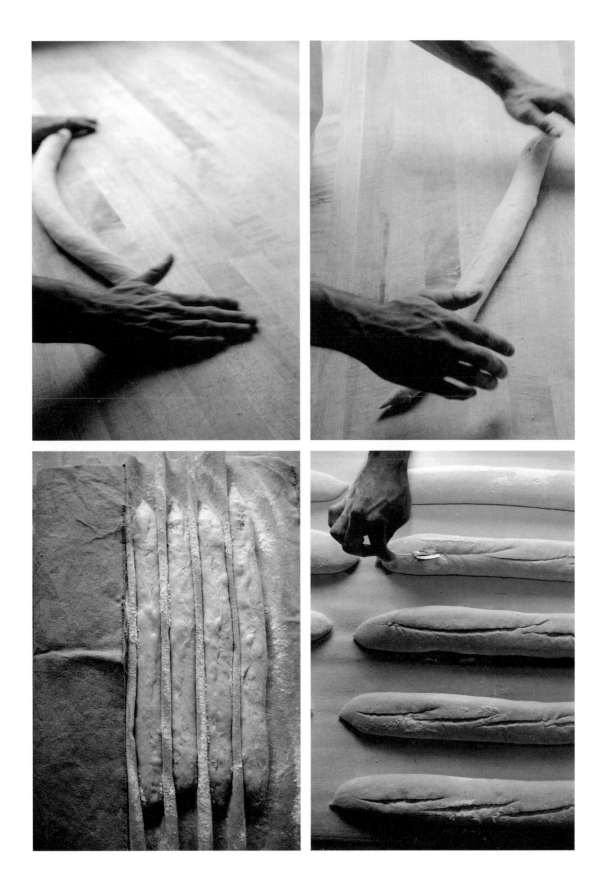

oven is to place a rimmed baking sheet lined with water-soaked kitchen towels in the bottom of the oven as it is preheating. As the oven heats, the moisture in the towels produces steam. Ideally, you want the oven to be steaming for 15 minutes after you load the baguettes to bake. Take care to get the baguettes into the oven quickly and shut the door; the more steam that stays in the oven during the first part of baking, the better the oven spring, or volume, of the finished loaves. The steam will also help develop a thin, crisp crust with a slight sheen.

Using rice flour, dust a pizza peel and dust the seam side of the baguettes. Holding the towel, flip each loaf onto a hand peel and then slide onto the pizza peel. Place the loaves side by side on the peel about 2 inches apart. With a double-edged razor, score each loaf down the center with a series of slightly overlapping lines. Make sure your oven is fully saturated with steam; you'll notice steam escaping from openings around the oven. Open the oven door, slide the baguettes onto the baking stone, and quickly shut the door to retain as much steam as possible. Immediately reduce the oven temperature to 475°F.

Once the baguettes start to color, after about 15 minutes, carefully remove the pan with the kitchen towels, which should be dry. Continue to bake the loaves until a deep golden color, 10 to 15 minutes. Serve warm from the oven or let cool on a rack.

Tordu

A rustic variation on the baguette, the tordu, meaning "twisted," resembles the gnarled trunk of a grapevine and is rarely found in bakeshops in the United States. The loaves of the "awesome baker" on the coast of France near Bordeux were my introduction to the tordu, which remains one of the most elegant shapes expressed in bread form.

Makes 2 or 3 loaves

1 recipe Baguette dough (page 126)

Prepare the baguette dough according to the recipe. After shaping the baguettes, put them on the flour-dusted towel and let rest for 5 minutes.

Holding each end of the dough, twist it in opposite directions as if wringing out a towel. Return the loaves to the floured towel and let rise for 2 to 2½ hours before baking.

Do not score the loaves. Bake as directed for the baguettes.

Fendu

The *fendu* shape, also called a *pistolet*, is not scored prior to baking and opens along the creased seam prepared carefully with rice flour as is our custom. I prefer the look of a final loaf that has not opened perfectly along the crease and, instead, sets its own expression during the final turn in the oven.

Makes 2 or 3 loaves

1 recipe Baguette dough (page 126)

Prepare the baguette dough according to the recipe. After the bulk fermentation is complete, divide the dough and let it rest as directed. Then, working with one dough rectangle at a time, fold the third of the dough closest to you up and over the middle third. Holding the ends of the dough, stretch it slightly. Fold the right third of the dough over the middle of the dough, and then fold the left third over the middle and the previous fold. Next, fold the third of the dough farthest from you over the middle as if closing the flap of an envelope. Press on this flap to develop tension in the dough. Using your palms and fingers together, roll the dough toward you; with each successive roll, press with the outer edge of your palms and fingers to further develop tension in the dough. You should end up with a squat oval of dough with the seam facing down.

cont'd

Using rice flour, dust the loaf lengthwise down the center. Push the wooden handle of a bench knife all the way through the dough until it touches the work surface. Again using the bench knife, flip the loaf onto a flour-dusted kitchen towel so that the seam is facing up. Let rise for 2 to 3 hours.

Do not score the loaves. Bake as directed for baguettes.

Fougasse

A traditional southern French flatbread, *fougasse* can be flavored with herbs, olives, and lardons (fried bacon or pork belly), and cut to resemble a leaf or ladder just before sliding onto the hearth to bake. The dough is pressed into a rectangular shape as for focaccia, and a bench knife is used to make swift, decisive cuts in the dough on the peel before it's cast onto the hearth to bake.

The variation shown above is a plain dough version of *fougasse*. If you want to flavor the bread with herbs, olives, or lardons, incorporate the ingredients early in the bulk rise, after the first turn, following the directions for the variations on Basic Country Bread (pages 88 to 93). The just-baked *fougasse* can be brushed with olive oil and seasoned with salt and fresh or dried herbs after it's pulled from the oven to suit your taste.

cont'd

Makes 2 or 3 loaves

1 recipe Baguette dough (page 126)

Prepare the baguette dough according to the recipe. After the bulk fermentation is complete, divide the dough and let it rest as directed. Then, working with one dough rectangle at a time, fold the third of the dough closest to you up and over the middle third. Holding the ends of the dough, stretch it slightly. Fold the right third of the dough over the middle of the dough, and then fold the left third over the middle and the previous fold. Next, fold the third of the dough farthest from you over the middle as if closing the flap of an envelope. Press on this flap to develop tension in the dough. Using your palms and fingers together, roll the dough toward you; with each successive roll, press with the outer edge of your palms and fingers to further develop tension in the dough. You should end up with a slightly rectangular cylinder with the seam facing down. Using a bench knife, flip the loaf onto a flour-dusted kitchen towel so that the seam is facing up. Press out the dough until it is about 1½ inches thick. Let rise for 2 to 3 hours.

Transfer the fougasse loaves to a flour-dusted pizza peel. Using the bench knife, make a pattern of cuts in the dough, pushing the knife until it touches the peel and being careful not to cut through the edge of the dough. Stretch the cut areas to create openings. Bake as directed for baguettes.

English Muffin

As anyone raised on Thomas', my ideal English muffin is a griddle cake with a tender, open-textured crumb—perfect for pooling melting butter and home-made jam.

The obvious choice for the open texture I wanted was the basic country dough. Early testing achieved decent results. But it was clear I needed a slightly firmer dough to withstand cutting it and transferring it to the griddle while maintaining the characteristic round shape. The baguette dough was just right—firm enough to hold its shape and supple enough to give an open-textured, tender crumb, with extra spring from the poolish to make an overall lighter muffin.

I also wanted the technique and production schedule to work so that the dough would be ready to cook in the morning, the natural time one would make English muffins. Ideally, you would be able to make the dough the day before and store it in the refrigerator overnight so that it could be cooked anytime the next morning. English muffins are great toasted and could be made a day or two ahead, but there is nothing quite like an English muffin fresh off the griddle.

The key to achieving English muffins with an open crumb is to keep the dough handling gentle and to a minimum. The dough needs a sufficient bulk rise to develop flavor and pockets of air throughout.

Makes 12 to 14 English muffins

1 recipe Baguette dough (page 126)
Mix of rice and all-purpose wheat flour for dusting
Cornmeal (optional)
1 cup (1 stick) unsalted butter

Prepare the baguette dough according to the recipe. Allow the dough to undergo bulk fermentation for 3 to 4 hours. During this time, give the dough one or two light turns.

Place a kitchen towel on a rimmed baking sheet and dust with rice flour mixture. Be sure to flour the towel well. Otherwise, the muffins can stick, and if they are forced later from the towel, they will be misshapen and will not rise evenly when cooked. Although the use of cornmeal rather than flour gives English muffins their trademark look, it tends to burn when the muffins are cooked on the griddle.

After the bulk fermentation is complete, turn the dough onto the well-floured towel and let relax for 10 minutes. Dust the top with rice flour mix mixture and press the dough from the middle outward until it is ¾ to 1 inch thick. Evenness is more important than exact thickness. Cover with a kitchen towel and place in the refrigerator to complete the rising overnight.

Remove the dough from refrigerator about 30 minutes before cooking the muffins. Have ready a cast-iron skillet or griddle, a 3-inch round cookie cutter, and a spatula. Melt the butter in a small saucepan over high heat. When the butter begins to boil, pour it through a fine-mesh strainer into a heatproof cup. The butter does not need to be perfectly clear; removing most of the milk solids is sufficient to prevent scorching.

Heat the skillet over medium-low heat. Add just enough of the clarified butter to coat the bottom of the pan. Using the cookie cutter, cut rounds from the dough as you are ready to place them in the pan. Carefully pick up each round and lay it in the pan. A 12-inch skillet will hold two or three rounds. After 2 minutes, the muffins will puff nearly 2 inches high. Don't worry if they puff unevenly—they will even out when turned. When the undersides are golden brown, use the spatula to turn the muffins. Press them lightly with the spatula so that they lie flat. Cook until the second sides are golden brown, 2 to 3 minutes more. The tops and bottoms should be golden brown and crisp, and the edges light and soft.

Remove the muffins from the skillet and serve warm or let cool on a rack. Wipe the skillet clean and repeat to cook the remaining muffins. If you like, dust the finished muffins with cornmeal.

To serve, split the muffins with a fork and pull apart. The muffins will keep at room temperature in a bread box or wrapped in waxed paper to retain moisture for 2 to 3 days as long as you toast them before serving. English muffins freeze well in a freezer-proof container. Thaw at room temperature for 2 hours and toast to restore.

BRIOCHE AND CROISSANT

"I like bread, and I like butter—but I like bread with butter best."

This quote from Sarah Weiner was written as an ode to her favorite things. Sarah was seven years old when she declared this—a precocious child; the daughter of a fellow baker and dear friend, Mariana Weiner, she summed up the opinion of a nation.

The alchemy of bread and butter: within the French tradition, there are masterful ways of combining the two to achieve outsized effect.

Two notable techniques are addressed here: brioche and croissant. Both begin as basic bread doughs. For brioche dough, butter is incorporated into a lean bread dough to make a smooth and silky enriched dough. Croissant dough, with butter enveloped between layers of the bread dough, is an exquisite transformation of bread and butter into a delicately layered, crisp and flaky pastry.

Traditionally, brioche dough was made with natural leaven. Croissant dough likely used a combination of natural leaven and yeast. As in the baguette recipe, this is a variation of a technique dating back more than a century, called *levain de pâte*. The lack of bakers skilled in using natural leaven led to an almost complete loss of this technique for making enriched, sweet breads. It's a shame, as the young leaven technique yields extraordinary results.

The savory element that the combined natural leaven and poolish bring to the dough creates a perfect balance within the rich, buttery nature of these pastries. The keeping qualities of croissants and brioche are improved by the use of leaven and poolish; even when a few days old, they restore well in a toaster oven.

The dough for both croissants and brioche is similar to baguette dough; milk replaces the water, and in the case of brioche, eggs form the main liquid portion. Each recipe uses a combination of a young leaven and poolish. Sugar is added to balance the flavor with subtle sweetness; a small amount of active dry yeast ensures adequate oven spring and a light texture for these rich doughs.

BRIOCHE

Brioche is the only dough in this book requiring the use of an electric mixer. A long, steady amount of mixing is required to fully incorporate the butter. The quantity of butter added to the dough is 45 percent of the total weight of the flour. This brioche has many uses sweet and savory, and keeps well for days.

This recipe yields nearly 4 pounds of brioche dough. Because of the addition of active dry yeast, the dough holds up well to freezing in a freezer-proof container. If you are using frozen dough, move to the refrigerator the night before you plan to use it and let it thaw overnight. You will need molds for baking the

brioche. At Tartine, we use loaf pans. Coffee cans work well, too. Whatever molds you choose, unless they have a nonstick surface, brush with melted butter or olive oil to prevent sticking.

Makes 4 to 6 brioche loaves

POOLISH

200 grams all-purpose flour

200 grams water (75°F)

3 grams active dry yeast

LEAVEN

1 tablespoon mature starter (see page 45)

220 grams all-purpose flour

220 grams water (80°F)

BRIOCHE

INGREDIENT	QUANTITY	BAKER'S PERCENTAGE
Bread Flour	1,000 g (1 kilogram)	100
Salt	25 grams	2.5
Sugar	120 grams	12
Active Dry Yeast	10 grams	1
Large Eggs	500 grams	50
Whole Milk	240 grams	24
Leaven	300 grams	30
Poolish	400 grams	40
Unsalted Butter	450 grams	45

EGG WASH

2 large egg yolks

1 teaspoon heavy cream

To make the poolish, in a bowl, mix the flour, water, and yeast. Let stand for 3 to 4 hours at a warm room temperature (75° to 80°F) or overnight in the refrigerator.

To make the leaven, place the mature starter in a bowl. Feed with the flour and the water, following step 1 on page 47.

The poolish and the leaven are ready when they pass the float test. Drop a small amount of the poolish and the leaven into water. If either sinks, it is not ready to use and needs more time to ferment.

About 30 minutes before you are ready to mix the brioche dough, remove the butter from the refrigerator and let soften at room temperature until it is pliable but still cool.

To mix the brioche dough, attach the dough hook to a stand mixer. Place the flour, salt, sugar, and yeast in the mixing bowl. Add the eggs, milk, leaven, and poolish and mix on low speed until combined, 3 to 5 minutes; stop the mixer halfway through and scrape down the sides of the bowl with a rubber spatula. Let the dough rest in the bowl for 15 to 20 minutes.

After the dough has rested, mix it on medium to high speed until it releases from the sides of the bowl, 6 to 8 minutes. This indicates that the dough is sufficiently developed to begin incorporating the butter. Make sure the butter is soft and pliable but still cool and not melted.

Cut the butter into ½-inch pieces. With the mixer on medium speed, add the pieces of butter one at a time to the middle of the bowl where the dough hook meets the dough. Continue until the butter is incorporated. The dough will be silky smooth and homogenous, with no visible bits of butter.

Transfer the dough to a bowl and set in a cool place (70°F) for 2 hours for the bulk fermentation. During the first hour, give the dough two turns, following step 5 on page 54. During the second hour, give it one turn. This is a very forgiving dough. If you want to shape the dough the next day, place the dough in a freezer-proof container after the 2-hour bulk fermentation and freeze for 3 to 5 hours, then transfer to the refrigerator and store there overnight. If you are shaping the dough and baking the brioche the same day, make sure that the bulk fermentation occurs in a cool place, or the butter will melt out of the dough, and the dough will feel greasy.

Just before shaping the dough, coat the brioche molds with butter. Use a dough spatula to pull the dough from the bowl onto an unfloured work surface. With a bench knife, cut the dough into four to six equal pieces. Shape each piece into a loaf following the instructions in step 6 on page 56.

Place the shaped dough in the molds and let rise in a draft-free place at a warm room temperature (75°F) for 1½ to 2 hours.

Preheat the oven to 450°F.

To make the egg wash, in a small bowl, stir together the egg yolks and cream. Brush the top of each loaf with the egg wash. Bake until the loaves are golden brown, 35 to 40 minutes. Unmold and let cool on a wire rack. The loaves should feel light in the hand and have the aroma of browned butter.

OLIVE OIL BRIOCHE

This version of brioche comes from southern France, where olive oil was once more readily available than butter. While butter brioche is a rich delicacy, olive oil brioche is its sun-bleached cousin: strongly flavored and tied to the land of its origin. Flavoring with orange blossom water, while not essential, is traditional and delicious.

The assertiveness of the oil depends on the variety you choose. For the version we make at Tartine, we like to taste the olive oil in the finished bread, so we use a strong-flavored extra-virgin oil. Though exceptional, the flavor is not nearly as distinct from the butter brioche as you might expect. Olive oil brioche is a fine substitute in any recipe that calls for brioche.

The brioche dough can be baked the same day or retarded in the refrigerator overnight; any dough that you do not use can be frozen for up to a week.

Makes 4 to 6 brioche loaves

BRIOCHE

INGREDIENT	QUANTITY	BAKER'S PERCENTAGE
Poolish	400 grams	40
Leaven	300 grams	30
Bread Flour	1,000 grams (1 kilogram)	100
Salt	25 grams	2.5
Active Dry Yeast	15 grams	1.5
Large Eggs	500 grams	50
Whole Milk	240 grams	24
Honey	160 grams	16
Orange Blossom Water	50 grams	5
Extra-virgin Olive Oil	450 grams	45

EGG WASH

2 large egg yolks

1 teaspoon heavy cream

Prepare the poolish and leaven as directed in the Brioche recipe, pages 144 to 149.

cont'd

Attach the dough hook to a stand mixer. Place the flour, salt, and yeast in the mixing bowl. Add the eggs, milk, leaven, poolish, honey, and orange blossom water and mix on low speed until combined, 3 to 5 minutes; stop the mixer halfway through and scrape down the sides of the bowl with a rubber spatula. Let the dough rest in the bowl for 15 to 20 minutes.

After the dough has rested, mix it on medium to high speed until it releases from the sides of the bowl, 6 to 8 minutes. This indicates that the dough is sufficiently developed to begin incorporating the olive oil. With the mixer on medium speed, add the oil in a steady stream, stopping intermittently to allow the dough to incorporate the oil. After all the oil is incorporated, the dough will be silky smooth and homogenous.

Transfer the dough to a bowl and set in a cool place (70°F) for 2 hours for the bulk fermentation. During the first hour, give the dough two turns following step 5 on page 54. During the second hour, give it one turn.

This is a very forgiving dough. If you want to shape the dough the next day, place the dough in a freezer-proof container after the 2-hour bulk fermentation, freeze for 3 to 5 hours, and then transfer to the refrigerator and store there overnight.

Just before shaping the dough, coat the brioche molds with butter. Use a dough spatula to pull the dough from the bowl onto an unfloured work surface. With a bench knife, cut the dough into four to six equal pieces. Shape each piece into a loaf following the instructions in step 6 on page 56.

Place the shaped dough in the molds and let rise in a draft-free place at a warm room temperature (75°F) for 1½ to 2 hours.

Preheat the oven to 450°F.

To make the egg wash, in a small bowl, stir together the egg yolks and cream. Brush the top of each loaf with the egg wash. Bake until the loaves are golden brown, 35 to 40 minutes. Unmold and let cool on a wire rack. The loaves should feel light in the hand and have the aroma of olive oil and orange blossoms.

VARIATIONS ON BRIOCHE

Beignets

Our beignets—brioche dough fried quickly, bathed in lemon glaze, and then tossed with maple-glazed pecans—use components of other preparations that we always have on hand at Tartine. The fritters are convenient to make if you are already preparing brioche dough. Only 200 grams of the dough need to be set aside for making the beignets.

Makes about 12 beignets

All-purpose flour for dusting

200 grams Brioche dough (page 144)

MAPLE PECANS

2 tablespoons maple syrup

2 tablespoons corn syrup

2 tablespoons granulated sugar

⅛ teaspoon salt

2 cups pecans

LEMON GLAZE

Grated zest and juice of 3 lemons (about ⅔ cup juice)

1 cup granulated sugar

½ cup powdered sugar

Olive or safflower oil for deep-frying

cont'd

Shape the beignets about 2 hours before serving. Lightly flour the dough and the work surface. Roll the dough into a cylinder about ½ inch in diameter. If the dough feels as if it will not stretch further, let it rest for 10 minutes and continue rolling. Transfer the dough to a cutting board and set in a draft-free place or cover with a kitchen towel. Let rise until the dough looks soft and inflated, 1 to 2 hours.

Meanwhile, to make the maple pecans, preheat the oven to 400°F. Line a rimmed baking sheet with parchment paper. In a bowl, stir together the maple syrup, corn syrup, granulated sugar, and salt. Add the pecans and toss to coat with the syrup mixture. Spread the pecans in an even layer on the baking sheet. Bake the nuts until the syrup glaze begins to bubble and then stir the nuts every few minutes to disperse the glaze. The nuts are done when the glaze has thickened and the bubbles have slowed, about 15 minutes. Let cool completely on the pan. The cooled nuts should be crisp. Finely chop the nuts.

To make the lemon glaze, combine the lemon zest and juice and the granulated and powdered sugars in a bowl and stir to combine.

Pour oil into a heavy, high-sided pan to a depth of 2 to 3 inches. Heat the oil over medium-high heat until it registers 375°F on a deep-frying thermometer.

When deep-frying, it's best to set up your prep area like an assembly line so you can work safely and efficiently. Set a rack near the stove and under it place a layer or two of paper towels. You also need a slotted spoon to turn the beignets and remove them from the oil after frying. Cut the dough on the diagonal into pieces about 2 inches long or as you prefer and then place near the stove.

Carefully slip four pieces of dough into the hot oil and fry until golden brown, about 1 minute. Using the slotted spoon, turn the dough and fry until brown on the second side, about 1 minute.

Carefully remove the beignets from the oil and transfer to the wire rack. Fry the remaining pieces of dough, checking the temperature of the oil intermittently. If necessary, allow a couple of minutes for the oil to return to 375°F in between batches.

When the beignets are cool enough to handle, dip them in the lemon glaze and then in the chopped pecans, coating them evenly. The pecans should stick to the beignet, and the glaze will harden slightly as the beignets continue to cool. Serve warm or at room temperature.

Brioche Lardon

This savory brioche was inspired by one of many extraordinary bites I've enjoyed from Amaryll Schwertner's hands at Boulette's Larder in San Francisco's Ferry Building. The bread, which keeps well for a few days, is best eaten toasted with peach or plum jam—or, as Amaryll served it, with fig conserve. Split and toasted, the lardon bun holds promise of a handsome fried egg sandwich.

Makes 2 loaves

2 pounds Brioche dough (page 144)

8 ounces thick-cut smoked bacon or pancetta, cut into batons

¾ cup hazelnuts, toasted and coarsely chopped

1 small bunch fresh thyme, stems removed

Grated zest of 1 orange

1 teaspoon freshly ground pepper

2 tablespoons unsalted butter, melted

cont'd

When making the brioche dough, remove 2 pounds of the dough from the mixing bowl prior to bulk fermentation.

In a wide bowl, stir together the bacon, hazelnuts, thyme leaves, orange zest, and pepper. Add to the brioche dough and, using your hands, mix to combine.

Let rise at a warm room temperature (about 80°F) for about 2 hours. Give the dough one turn per hour, following step 5 on page 54. Brush the inside of four tall ring molds, each 4 inches in diameter, with melted butter. Line a baking sheet with parchment paper. Place the prepared molds on the baking sheet. Turn the dough out onto a work surface and divide into four pieces. Form each piece into a round and place in a ring mold.

Let rise at a warm room temperature (about 80°F) for 1½ to 2 hours.

Preheat the oven to 425°F. Bake the brioche until golden brown, 35 to 40 minutes. Unmold onto a wire rack. Serve fresh or toasted.

Kugelhopf

A traditional Alsatian brioche bread, kugelhopf is made to celebrate any number of different occasions. A kugelhopf mold, unglazed on the exterior, is generally used to bake the bread. A metal bundt pan—while straying from tradition—works perfectly well. You can serve the kugelhopf fresh or, as is the custom, a day or two after it is baked.

Makes 1 kugelhopf

2 pounds Brioche dough (page 144)

½ cup dried currants

1 cup Schnapps, marc, or grappa

1 cup dried apricots, chopped

¾ cup pistachios, toasted

½ teaspoon ground cardamom

1 tablespoon orange blossom water

½ cup unsalted butter, melted

12 almonds

¼ cup confectioners' sugar

cont'd

When making the brioche dough, remove 2 pounds of the dough from the mixing bowl prior to bulk fermentation.

A day ahead, place the currants in a small bowl and pour in the liquor. Let soak overnight. Drain, reserving the soaking liquor.

In a wide bowl, stir together the soaked currants, apricots, pistachios, cardamom, and orange blossom water. Add to the brioche dough and, using your hands, mix to combine.

Let rise at a warm room temperature (about 80°F) for about 2 hours. Give the dough one turn per hour, following step 5 on page 54. Turn the dough out onto a work surface and shape into a round. Brush a kugelhopf mold with some of the melted butter and place an almond in each top crease around the crown. Make a hole in the center of the dough and place the dough, seam-side up, in the mold.

Let rise at a warm room temperature (about 80°F) for 1½ to 2 hours.

Preheat the oven to 425°F. Bake the kugelhopf until golden brown, 35 to 40 minutes. Unmold onto a wire rack and brush with melted butter while warm. Dust with some of the confectioner's sugar and brush with the reserved soaking liquor. If serving the bread a day or two later, wrap the cooled kugelhopf and store at room temperature. Dust with confectioner's sugar again before serving.

CROISSANTS

To get from the baguette dough to croissant dough, this recipe starts with virtually the same lean dough but substitutes milk for the water and adds a small amount of sugar. The butter is enveloped in the dough after the dough is mixed, using a lamination process that creates alternating layers of dough and butter. The process sounds more complicated than it is—but it results in the crisp, light, multilayered texture you expect in the classic croissant. A well-made croissant will give one pause, a moment to reflect on the pétit engineering marvel set before you.

Makes 14 to 16 croissants

POOLISH

200 grams all-purpose flour

200 grams water (75°F)

3 grams active dry yeast

LEAVEN

1 tablespoon mature starter (page 45)

220 grams all-purpose flour

220 grams water (80°F)

CROISSANTS

INGREDIENT	QUANTITY	BAKER'S PERCENTAGE
Whole Milk	450 grams	45
Leaven	300 grams	30
Poolish	400 grams	40
Bread Flour	1,000 grams (1 kilogram)	100
Salt	28 grams	2.8
Sugar	85 grams	8.5
Active Dry Yeast	10 grams	1
Cold Unsalted Butter	400 grams	40

½ cup all-purpose flour

EGG WASH

2 large egg yolks

1 teaspoon heavy cream

cont'd

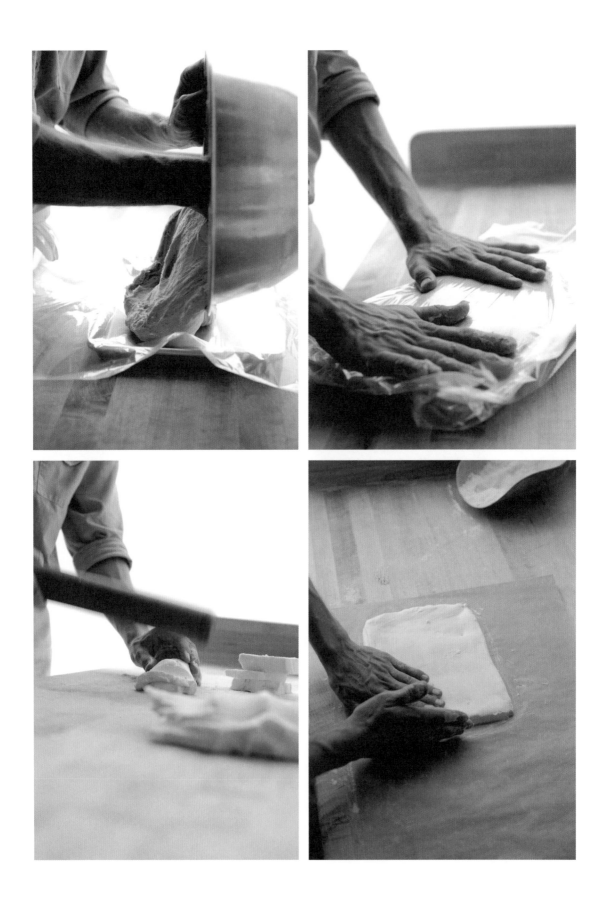

To make the poolish, in a bowl, mix the flour, water, and yeast. Let stand for 3 to 4 hours at a warm room temperature (75° to 80°F) or overnight in the refrigerator.

To make the leaven, place the mature starter in a bowl. Feed with the flour and water, following step 1 on page 47.

The poolish and the leaven are ready when they pass the float test. Drop a small amount of the poolish and the leaven into water. If either sinks, it is not ready to use and needs more time to ferment.

Before mixing the croissant dough, remove the milk from the refrigerator and let it warm to room temperature.

Pour the milk into a large mixing bowl. Add the leaven and the poolish and stir to disperse. Add the flour, salt, sugar, and yeast. Using your hands, mix thoroughly until no bits of dry flour remain. Let the dough rest for 25 to 40 minutes.

Follow step 4 on page 52 to transfer the dough to a clear container and let the dough undergo bulk fermentation at a warm room temperature (75° to 80°F) for 1½ hours. Give the dough one turn ever 30 minutes, following step 5 on page 54.

Transfer the dough to a plastic bag, press to flatten it into a rectangle, and chill it in the refrigerator for 2 to 3 hours.

Have ready a rolling pin and the ½ cup all-purpose flour. Prepare the butter just before you are ready to laminate the dough and butter. Cut the cold butter into cubes. Pound the cubes with the rolling pin until they come together into a single cohesive mass. Incorporate the ½ cup flour into the butter as you pound. You want the butter mass to be the same consistency as the dough. The goal is to make the stiff, cold butter pliable without warming it.

Mold the butter into a rectangle measuring roughly 8 by 12 inches, place on a sheet of parchment paper, and keep cool. Take care not to let the butter block chill to the point that it is no longer pliable; otherwise you will have to pound it again. You want the butter to maintain its spreadable quality, as it will be rolled out thinner and thinner, sandwiched between layers of the dough.

When you are ready to begin lamination, place the dough on a stable work surface dusted with flour and roll out to a rectangle measuring roughly 12 by 20 inches. Arrange the rectangle so that it is horizontal. Working quickly, place the butter block in the center of the dough. Fold the right and left portions of the dough over the butter as if you are folding a letter. Immediately turn the dough 90 degrees and roll it again into a rectangle about 12 by 20 inches. Do the letter fold again, taking care to keep the edges of the rectangle even and unbroken. This is your first "turn."

cont'd

Wrap the dough in parchment paper and refrigerate for 1 hour to allow the dough to relax before giving it the second turn. If you rest the dough too long in the refrigerator, the butter will harden. If that happens, remove the dough and let it warm up for 15 minutes before giving the next turn.

Clean the work surface and dust with flour. Set the dough on the floured surface and roll out to a 12-by-20-inch rectangle. Again arrange the rectangle so that it is horizontal and fold the dough as if folding a letter, keeping the edges even. This is your second turn. Refrigerate the dough for 1 hour to allow it to relax without letting the butter harden.

Repeat to complete a third turn. You will have a rectangle of dough about 8 by 12 inches and 2 inches thick. This is called a block. Wrap the block in plastic wrap or parchment paper, place in the freezer, and chill for 1 to 2 hours.

If you intend to finish the croissants the next morning, leave the block in the freezer until just before you retire and then transfer it to the refrigerator. The dough will be ready to roll out and shape in the morning. You can store the block in the freezer, in freezer-proof wrap, for up to 3 days. Remember to transfer the block to the refrigerator the night before you plan to use it.

When you are ready to shape the croissants, line two baking sheets with parchment paper. Roll the dough into a rectangle approximately 18 by 24 inches and about ½ inch thick. Cut it in half to create two long rectangles each 9 by 24 inches. Using a knife, cut each rectangle into six to eight equal-sized triangles. Roll up each triangle, beginning at the widest side. Place the croissants on the prepared sheets, spacing them at least 1½ inches apart. Let rise at a warm room temperature (75° to 80°F) for about 2 hours. The croissants are ready to bake when they are 50 percent larger than their original size. They will be firm but puffed up.

You can also retard the final rise. This works well if you shape the croissants in the evening and want to bake them in the morning. Arrange them on the parchment-lined baking sheets. Wrap the sheets loosely with plastic wrap to keep the dough from forming a skin and refrigerate.

Preheat the oven to 425°F.

To make the egg wash, in a small bowl, stir together the egg yolks and cream. Brush the top of each croissant with the egg wash. Bake until the croissants are deep golden brown, crisp, and flaky, about 30 minutes. Serve warm or let cool on the pan. If necessary, reheat to serve.

CHAPTER 4

Days-Old Bread

LIZ, ERIC, NATE, AND I ALL FOUND OUR WAY to baking through the savory kitchen, as did Melissa Roberts, who has managed the Tartine pastry kitchen for years.

Bread is our staple. We eat it hot from the oven, snack on it while we make dinner, and serve it at the table. We toast it for breakfast and make sandwiches for lunch. The large loaves are often eaten over a few days.

In every place bread is a staple, resourceful cooks have found ways to incorporate it into a meal, wasting nothing. In this rich tradition, there are vastly more uses for stale bread than hot sandwiches and toast.

The thirty-plus recipes in this chapter are some of our favorite ways to make a meal from our days-old bread. All of the breads we use here are in the book for you to make. That said, you can use any bread you like for these preparations. The list began with things I had eaten over the years, which had been idealized in memory. Many are classic recipes we used as a starting point and made to suit our tastes.

One recipe daily: each morning, we discussed the food we'd make. While Lori or Nate mixed the dough, I went to the market. Midway through the bread shift, Eric broke away to prep and cook some test plates for tasting. After the day's bread was pre-shaped and during the bench rest, we considered how we wanted to present the dish for the book. Test plates were eaten for dinner. If we weren't satisfied with what we got—we made it over again the next day.

Long summer days provided evening light while we cooked and photographed the final dish. Afterwards, we finished shaping the day's bread, fed the starters, and shut off the lights.

There is no end to the uses of old bread, and new ideas kept coming. When we made the Trouble Affogato (page 277), after a nonstop season on this daily schedule, it seemed a fitting end to our feast.

These recipes are a starting point.

FRESH FAVA PANZANELLA

Open a bottle of wine and invite your friends into the kitchen early to help shell the beans. After the beans are prepared, the rest of this simple, flavorful salad comes together quickly.

The amount of vinaigrette may seem excessive, but it is used to dress both the croutons and the vegetables. Panzanella traditionally calls for stale bread soaked ahead of time in water, pressed dry, and then tossed and dressed with the other ingredients. Instead, we use our fried bread croutons. Once the croutons are dressed, the exterior softens slightly, leaving the contrasting interior crunch intact. *Serves 4 to 6*

1 red onion, cut into slices ¼ inch thick

½ cup red wine vinegar

4 pounds fava beans, shelled (yields about 4 cups)

Croutons (page 193), made from 4 slices day-old Basic Country Bread

1 bunch mint, stems removed

LEMON VINAIGRETTE

Grated zest and juice of 2 lemons

1 teaspoon sugar

1 cup olive oil

¼ teaspoon salt

Place the onion slices in a bowl and pour the vinegar over the slices. Add just enough water to cover the slices completely. Set aside for 30 minutes. The onions will soften slightly and take on a bright pink hue.

Meanwhile, bring a pot of water to a boil. Fill a bowl with ice water and place it near the stove. Add the fava beans to the boiling water and cook for 1 minute. Drain and transfer to the ice water to cool. Peel the opaque outer layer from each bean.

In a serving bowl, combine the fava beans, croutons, and mint leaves. Remove the onions from the vinegar and add to the bowl.

To make the vinaigrette, in a small bowl, stir together the lemon zest and juice, sugar, and olive oil. Season to taste with the salt, adding it a pinch at a time. Pour the vinaigrette over the salad and toss. Let stand for 1 minute before serving.

TOMATO PANZANELLA

Tomatoes with bread, artichokes roasted in olive oil, cucumbers, and shaved Parmesan combine to make a late summer staple. Absorbed by the croutons, the tomato vinaigrette is the hidden star of this quick salad. The tomato seeds carry the flavor of the fruit and add body to the dressing. *Serves 4 to 6*

ROASTED ARTICHOKE CROUTONS
Red wine vinegar or sherry vinegar

2 pounds baby artichokes

6 tablespoons olive oil

Salt

4 thick slices day-old Basic Country Bread (page 45), torn into large pieces

4 ounces fresh Parmesan cheese

TOMATO VINAIGRETTE
4 ripe heirloom tomatoes

½ red onion, finely diced

3 tablespoons red wine vinegar or sherry vinegar

¼ teaspoon salt

1 cup olive oil

1 English cucumber

1 bunch basil, stems removed

Preheat the oven to 400°F. Fill a large bowl with water and add a generous splash of vinegar. Remove the tough outer leaves from each artichoke until you reach the tender leaves surrounding the heart. Cut the artichoke in half lengthwise and place the halves in the acidulated water.

Drain the artichokes, place in a bowl, and toss with 3 tablespoons of the olive oil and a pinch of salt. Arrange the artichoke halves cut-side down in a large skillet. In the same bowl, toss the bread pieces with the remaining 3 tablespoons olive oil and a pinch of salt. Place the bread on top of the artichokes, grate the cheese over all, and put the pan in the oven. Roast until the artichokes are crispy on the outside and tender on the inside and the bread is a deep golden brown, 15 to 20 minutes.

cont'd

Meanwhile, to make the vinaigrette, cut each tomato in half crosswise. Holding each half over a small bowl, gently squeeze it (as if juicing an orange) to release the seeds. Reserve the tomatoes. Add the onion, vinegar, and salt to the seeds, and stir to combine. Stir in the olive oil.

Cut the reserved tomato halves into 1-inch chunks. Peel the cucumber. Using a mandoline or vegetable peeler, cut the cucumber lengthwise into thin strips.

In a serving bowl, combine the artichokes, croutons, tomatoes, cucumber, and basil. Add the vinaigrette and toss. Let stand for 3 to 5 minutes before serving.

ESCALIVADA

A number of classic dishes inspired this variation of bread salad. After a morning at the market, I had on hand the right mix of Provençal vegetables for making a ratatouille. It was a late summer day, and the weather called for grilling. Although *bagna cauda*, a warm sauce of garlic, oil, and anchovies seemed the ideal accompaniment, cooler *anchoïade* held greater appeal. Eric and I grilled the vegetables over hot coals and dressed them with the *anchoïade*. I later read that, in the Catalan tradition, this preparation is called *escalivada*, a word that refers to cooking the vegetables over hot coals. The versatile *anchoïade* works well as a sauce for meat or fish and also eaten with fresh cheese such as ricotta. *Serves 4 to 6*

1 large Rosa Bianca or globe eggplant, cut lengthwise into slices ¼ inch thick

3 zucchini or other summer squash, cut lengthwise into slices ¼ inch thick

6 Gypsy peppers, halved and seeded

1 red or yellow onion, cut into slices ¼ inch thick

½ cup olive oil

4 thick slices day-old Basic Country Bread (page 45) or similar bread

ANCHOÏADE

2 cloves garlic

6 olive oil–packed anchovy fillets

½ cup walnuts

½ teaspoon coriander seeds

Grated zest and juice of 1 lemon

½ cup olive oil

1 tablespoon fresh marjoram leaves

1 teaspoon fresh thyme leaves

½ cup dried or dark Mission figs, chopped

Salt and freshly ground pepper

2 ripe heirloom tomatoes, cut into 1-inch chunks

2 cups mixed fresh flat-leaf parsley and basil leaves

8 to 10 fresh figs, halved (optional)

cont'd

Prepare a fire in a charcoal grill. Brush the eggplant, zucchini, peppers, and onion generously with olive oil. Grill the vegetables, turning as needed, until they soften and are slightly charred, 6 to 8 minutes. Remove to a bowl. Brush bread slices with olive oil and grill, turning as needed, until crisp and slightly charred, about 4 minutes. Remove to the bowl and cut each slice in half.

To make the *anchoïade*, place the garlic and anchovies in a mortar and, using a pestle, pound into a paste. Add the walnuts and coriander seeds and pound to incorporate into the paste. Transfer to a bowl and stir in the lemon zest and juice, olive oil, marjoram, thyme, and dried figs. Season with salt and pepper.

Arrange the tomatoes, bread, parsley, and basil together on a platter with the grilled vegetables and fresh figs (if using). Spoon the *anchoïade* over the top and serve.

BAGNET VERT

This traditional Italian condiment (pronounced BAHN-yet), is related to Spanish *salsa verde*, Italian *bagna cauda*, and Greek *skordalia*. Another sauce with many uses, it is traditionally eaten with boiled meats and is delicious with pretty much anything else—in this case, marinated anchovies. At Bar Tartine, we serve Bagnet Vert with Bolinas black cod, cilantro blossoms, and fennel tops. The incorporation of bread transforms the sauce into something much more substantial, a sublime combination of aromatic flavors bound with bread. *Serves 4 to 6*

MARINATED ANCHOVIES

1 tablespoon coriander seeds

Two 2-ounce cans olive oil–packed anchovy fillets, drained

Grated zest of 1 lemon

Red pepper flakes

½ cup olive oil

1 bunch cilantro blossoms for garnish (optional)

BAGNET VERT

2 cups torn day-old Basic Country Bread (page 45)

1 tablespoon red wine or sherry vinegar

½ cup water

2 cups fresh flat-leaf parsley leaves, roughly chopped

1 cup olive oil

1 tablespoon capers

4 olive oil–packed anchovy fillets

½ teaspoon salt

Cilantro blossoms (optional)

To make the marinated anchovies, in a small frying pan over medium heat, toast the coriander seeds, stirring occasionally, until you smell the toasty aroma and the seeds begin to smoke slightly, about 5 minutes. Transfer the seeds to a mortar and coarsely crack with a pestle. Arrange the anchovy fillets on a plate and sprinkle with the lemon zest, coriander seeds, and pepper flakes. Pour enough olive oil over the fillets to cover them. Let marinate for 4 hours or up to overnight.

cont'd

To make the *bagnet vert*, place the bread in a bowl and toss with the vinegar and water. Let soften for 5 to 10 minutes. Transfer the bread to a blender and add the parsley, olive oil, capers, anchovies, and salt. Blend to a smooth puree. Add more water, a spoonful at a time, if the sauce is too thick to blend. Taste and season with salt if necessary.

Spoon the *bagnet vert* on plates and arrange the anchovies over the top. Garnish with the cilantro blossoms, if desired.

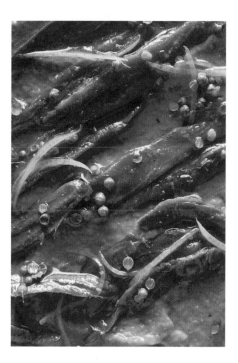

CROUTONS AND BREAD CRUMBS

A few years after starting out in Point Reyes, worn down from the labors of making bread in the preindustrial manner I had chosen, I found a short, handwritten note slipped under the bakeshop door. It was from Alice Waters. She had written to commend my work and convey appreciation for what I was doing. I had been inspired many times by her since I first began working in the kitchen, and her welcome note gave me a much-needed second wind at a pivotal time in my life.

Since those early days, Alice has generously offered her advice and support many times. While researching recipes for this chapter, I thought to ask if she could pass on any of her favorite ways of using days-old bread, hoping she might tell me about some obscure or antiquated recipe I had never heard of.

"Bread crumbs. We don't waste a scrap of bread at the restaurant," she said, referring to Chez Panisse, which she founded in 1971.

The significance of her advice took a day to sink in. At first, I figured she might have been too busy to suggest something more interesting. Then I began researching the trove of recipes that call for toasted bread crumbs. Whether used as a principal ingredient or as a garnish to add texture, bread crumbs are the most practical, versatile way to turn old bread into dinner. If you have stale bread, you have the makings of a substantial and thrifty meal. I went on to find many preparations, my favorites now, in which bread crumbs are an essential component.

A consummate visionary, Alice has so effectively promoted the sustainable connection of people with their food—where it comes from, how it's grown, and how it's prepared—that she has changed the way we eat, shifting us closer to the sources of our food. Not satisfied to reach only the dining public, she is working hard to affect change in the public school food system. Her dedication to these principles has never wavered.

Bread crumbs . . . I should have known.

CROUTONS

3 slices day-old bread, each 1 inch thick, torn into 1½-inch chunks

2 tablespoons olive oil

Salt

½ teaspoon *herbes de Provence* (optional)

To make croutons, preheat the oven to 400°F. In a bowl, toss the torn bread with the olive oil and a pinch of salt. If you are using the herbs, add them too. Spread the bread evenly on a baking sheet and bake until golden brown and crisp, about 15 minutes. Midway through the baking time, redistribute the croutons if they are coloring unevenly.

BREAD CRUMBS

To make bread crumbs, use your hands or a rolling pin to crush the croutons to the desired consistency. For a superfine texture, sift the crumbs through a sieve. If you like, add dried herbs fried in olive oil.

AIOLI AND ROUILLE

The word *Aioli* derives from two Spanish words meaning literally "garlic-oil." The most elemental version of this condiment is made by grinding garlic and salt into a paste. Moistened with olive oil and lemon, it turns to a sauce. To make a richer emulsion, I like to start with an egg yolk. Thickening with bread is an ancient custom that adds body to the sauce and is well-suited for use in soups.

Rouille is an aioli flavored with sweet red peppers, turning the sauce from golden yellow to deep red rust. Using the mortar and pestle is truly the most efficient way to make these sauces quickly and with the least amount of mess; the mortar is set on the table to serve. Both sauces are eaten with seafood, meats, and vegetables, and they are used to flavor or garnish soups and broths. *Makes 1 cup*

AIOLI
1 clove garlic, roughly chopped
Grated zest and juice of 1 lemon
¼ teaspoon salt
1 egg yolk
1 cup olive oil
1 slice day-old Basic Country Bread
(page 45)

ROUILLE
1 red bell pepper, peeled, roasted, and seeded
½ teaspoon red pepper flakes
1 recipe Aioli (at left)

To make the aioli, combine the garlic, lemon zest, and salt in a mortar and pound to a paste with a pestle. Add the egg yolk and ½ teaspoon of the lemon juice. Using the pestle, vigorously and consistently stir the mixture while adding the olive oil, drop by drop. After half of the oil is incorporated, the sauce should be creamy and smooth, the sign of a stable emulsion. Continuing to stir, add the remaining oil in a slow, thin stream. The more oil added, the thicker the sauce will be. Use as much of the remaining lemon juice as needed to flavor or thin the aioli. Transfer the aioli to a bowl. Place the bread in the mortar with a spoonful of remaining lemon juice or water. Using the pestle, pound the bread to a smooth paste. Add the aioli and stir to combine. Return to the bowl and serve.

To make rouille, combine the roasted pepper and red pepper flakes in the mortar and pound to a paste with the pestle. Stir into the aioli until smooth. Serve.

PAN CON TOMATE

Good toast with tomato, extra-special ham, and hard aged cheese is a summer favorite in tapas bars all over Spain. It doesn't get more *sencillo* than this. Naturally, use the best, very ripe tomatoes available and lots of olive oil to fry the bread properly. *Serves 1*

Olive oil—your best

1 slice fresh or day-old Basic Country Bread (page 45)

1 soft, ripe heirloom tomato, cut in half crosswise

1 thin slice dry-cured ham such as serrano

1 slice hard aged cheese such as Manchego

Pour ¼ inch of olive oil into a small skillet and heat over medium-high heat. Add the bread and fry until deep golden brown and very crisp, about 3 minutes. Turn and fry until deep golden brown and crisp on the other side. The rough surface of the bread forms a natural Microplane. Rub the cut side of the tomato halves across one side of the toasted bread until the pulp is shredded and the juice fills the holes in the bread with tomato puree. Top with the ham and cheese and serve.

LATE SUMMER BRUSCHETTA

The choice combination of ripe tomato and basil with garlic on toast is fresh again each summer with the arrival of the first tomatoes and basil tips of the season. Inspiration sets in quickly once the bounty of summer mounts; good flavors follow.

　　We start here with Italian tradition, adding flavors from Mexican street vendors in the neighborhood who season fresh fruit with chile, lime, and salt; shifting the profile in a way we like. If you are making the Eggplant and Charred Pepper Bruschetta (page 204) along with one of the others, start by preparing the eggplant so that it has time to roast and marinate. Toast the bread in the oven or fry in olive oil on the stove top in a skillet before topping. *Makes 6 large bruschetta per variation*

6 slices day-old Basic Country Bread　　Olive oil
(page 45)

To toast the bread in the oven, preheat the oven to 400°F. Arrange the bread on a baking sheet and brush with olive oil if desired. Toast until golden brown, 10 to 15 minutes. Alternatively, to fry the bread, pour ¼ inch of olive oil into a large skillet and heat over medium-high heat. Add the bread and fry until deep golden brown and very crisp, about 3 minutes. Turn and fry until deep golden brown and crisp on the second side.

TOMATO, MELON, AND CHILE BRUSCHETTA

LEMON VINAIGRETTE
Grated zest and juice of 2 lemons

½ teaspoon sugar, plus more as needed

1 cup olive oil

Salt

CHILE SALT
4 dried hot chiles

½ teaspoon salt

3 ripe heirloom tomatoes (about
1 pound), cut into ½-inch chunks

1 ripe melon (about 1 pound), peeled,
seeded, and cut into ½-inch chunks

½ cup fresh basil leaves, some left whole
and some torn

½ cup fresh mint leaves, some left whole
and some torn

6 slices toasted Basic Country Bread
(page 45)

To make the vinaigrette, in a bowl, stir together the lemon zest and juice,
½ teaspoon sugar, and the olive oil. Season with sugar and salt.

To make the chile salt, heat a small skillet over high heat. Add the chiles and press
down on them with a spatula. They will toast quickly, in about 3 minutes. Turn
the chiles and press with the spatula to toast on the second side for about 3 minutes. Transfer the chiles to a mortar; they will become brittle as they cool. Add
the salt and pound with a pestle until you get a mixture of powder and flakes.

In a bowl, combine tomatoes, melon, basil, and mint. Stir in a few spoonfuls of
lemon vinaigrette. Spoon the mixture on the toasted bread, sprinkle with the
chile salt, and serve.

SUMMER SQUASH AND PEA BRUSCHETTA

4 zucchini and summer squash
(about 2 pounds)

Salt

1 pound sugar snap peas (about 1 cup)

½ ripe melon, peeled, seeded, and cut
into ½-inch chunks

½ cup fresh mint leaves, some left
whole and some torn

Lemon Vinaigrette (facing page)

6 slices toasted Basic Country Bread
(page 45)

6 ounces fresh Parmesan cheese

Using a mandoline or a wide vegetable peeler, cut the squash lengthwise into
thin strips. Put the strips and a pinch of salt in a bowl and toss. Let stand for
5 to 10 minutes. Fresh squash is brittle, and the salt will draw out some of the
moisture and make it more pliable.

Add the peas, melon, and mint to the squash along with a few generous spoonfuls of lemon vinaigrette to dress.

Spoon the mixture on the toasted bread. Using a vegetable peeler, shave the
Parmesan over the bruschetta. Serve.

EGGPLANT AND CHARRED PEPPER BRUSCHETTA

SHERRY VINAIGRETTE

½ red onion

½ cup sherry vinegar

½ cup dried currants

2 tablespoons sugar

¼ teaspoon salt

½ cup olive oil

EGGPLANT

3 small eggplants (about 1 pound)

Olive oil

Salt

½ cup fresh basil leaves, some left whole and some torn

CHARRED PEPPERS

1 tablespoon olive oil

12 Padrón peppers

Salt

6 slices toasted Basic Country Bread (page 45)

To make the sherry vinaigrette, cut the onion into paper-thin slices. Place the slices in a bowl and add the vinegar, currants, sugar, and salt. Stir to combine and let stand for 5 minutes. The onions will turn bright pink. Add ½ cup olive oil.

To prepare the eggplant, preheat the oven to 400°F. Line a baking sheet with parchment paper or a rimmed nonstick liner.

Cut the eggplants lengthwise into slices ¼ inch thick. Generously brush both sides of each slice with olive oil and arrange on the prepared sheet in a single layer. Sprinkle liberally with salt. Bake until the slices are very soft, about 20 minutes. Let the eggplant slices cool and then transfer them to a shallow serving dish. Top with the basil leaves and pour the sherry vinaigrette over the slices. Let marinate for about 30 minutes before serving.

Char the peppers right before serving, making sure the kitchen is well ventilated. Place the 1 tablespoon oil in a skillet and heat over high heat. When the oil begins to smoke, add the peppers and cook, without moving them, for 1 minute. Shake the skillet so the peppers flip over, or turn them with a spatula. Cook on the second side for 1 minute. Season the peppers with a pinch of salt and transfer to the serving dish with the eggplant.

Spoon the eggplant and peppers onto the toasted bread. Moisten with the marinade and serve.

Raclette

The tradition of raclette began in Switzerland's Valais, but it is also popular in France's Savoy region. Liz and I found ourselves at many memorable late-night feasts in the French Alps, where we worked with Patrick LePort at his Boulangerie Savoyarde. These festive meals, generously prepared by the bakers, often ended with the first morning light.

We set a half wheel of raclette cheese to slowly melt on a slab of stone in front of an open fire. A specially made tool resembling a hoe is used to scrape the softened cheese and spread it on bread. Raclette is the name of both the tradition and the cheese—*racler* meaning "to scrape." The cheese is traditionally eaten with baked potatoes, pickled vegetables, strong mustard, cured meats, and copious *vin de Savoie*.

For outdoor occasions, do as Savoyard shepherds have done for generations: build a campfire, place a clean, flat rock close to the flame and set a portion of cheese on top with the cut side facing the heat. Let the cheese melt slowly and spread it on toasted bread.

Use about 6 ounces of cheese per person.

PICKLED SARDINES

Fresh sardines are a seasonal treat. We buy lots of them when they're available. Grilled and eaten with dressed shaved fennel and aioli, they make a fast and easy meal. To preserve the fish for eating over the week, we fillet and pickle them. Fresh pickled sardines on toast with crushed avocado is a favorite snack. Try frying the backbones in olive oil to make a crisp, delicious garnish. Greens for the herb salad we use at Tartine are grown by our friend Brooke at Little City Gardens, just a few doors from the bakery. *Serves 4 to 6*

12 fresh sardines

½ red onion, cut into ¼ inch strips

Grated zest and juice of 3 lemons

½ cup sugar

1 tablespoon salt

1 cup olive oil

1 orange, cut crosswise into slices ⅛ inch thick

¼ cup fresh marjoram leaves, some left whole and some torn

VINAIGRETTE

2 tablespoons olive oil

2 teaspoons Champagne vinegar

½ teaspoon finely chopped shallot

Salt and freshly ground pepper

HERB SALAD

1 cup arugula

¼ cup fresh flat-leaf parsley leaves

¼ cup fresh cilantro leaves and blossoms

¼ cup fresh basil tips

¼ cup fresh chervil leaves

¼ cup small fennel tops, roughly chopped

¼ cup chopped purslane

¼ cup sunflower petals

Olive oil

3 slices day-old Basic Country Bread (page 45), each about 1 inch thick

Garlic shoots, to taste

Fillet the sardines by making an incision in each fish along the length of the belly all the way to the tail. Remove the guts and rinse the fish under running water. Using your fingers, peel the flesh away from the backbone at the tail end. When the backbone is loose, pinch the tail and pull up and toward the head, teasing the bones from the flesh. Cut the fish down the middle to separate it into two fillets, and cut around each fillet to clean up the edges. Reserve the bones if you want to fry them later.

cont'd

Place the onion slices in a bowl, add the lemon zest and juice, and let stand for about 5 minutes. Stir in the sugar, salt, and olive oil. Layer half of the sardine fillets, orange slices, and marjoram in a shallow dish and pour half of the lemon–olive oil mixture over the top. Repeat with the remaining sardine fillets, orange slices, marjoram, and lemon–olive oil mixture . You can eat the sardines within a few minutes, when the lemon juice has barely begun to "cook" the fish. The longer the fillets stand in the liquid, the more thoroughly they pickle. You can keep the sardines covered in the liquid in the refrigerator for up to 1 week. The flavors of the marjoram and orange become stronger, and the flesh of the sardines becomes firmer the longer they are left in the liquid.

To make the vinaigrette, in a small bowl, whisk together the oil, vinegar, and shallot. Season with salt and pepper.

To make the herb salad, in a bowl, combine the arugula, parsley, cilantro, basil, chervil, fennel, purslane, and petals. Add the vinaigrette and toss to combine.

Pour ¼ inch of olive oil into a large skillet and heat over medium-high heat. Add the bread and fry until deep golden brown and very crisp, about 3 minutes. Turn and fry until deep golden brown and crisp on the second side.

Heat ½ cup olive oil in a small skillet over medium-high heat. When the oil is hot, add the sardine bones two at a time and fry until very crispy and brittle, about 2½ minutes. Remove from the oil and season with salt.

Serve the sardines on the fried bread and with the herb salad. Mashed ripe avocado and Crystal chile sauce are welcome additions.

SARDINES AND FRESH GARBANZO HUMMUS

Tinned sardines on toast and cold beer is a staple dinner eaten alone after a long shift. Here's another version for company. Fresh garbanzo beans are available only for a short season and are worth searching out. Dried garbanzos are a fine substitute. *Serves 2, with leftover hummus*

HUMMUS

2 pounds fresh garbanzo beans, shelled, or 1 pound dried garbanzos

3 cloves garlic, if using fresh garbanzos

1 teaspoon cumin seeds, toasted, if using dried garbanzos

3 tablespoons sesame tahini

12 fresh mint leaves, if using fresh garbanzos

Juice of 1 lemon

½ teaspoon salt

1 cup olive oil

Olive oil

2 slices fresh or day-old Whole-Wheat Bread (page 114)

1 hard-boiled egg

One 3.75-ounce can olive oil–packed sardines

½ cup chopped fresh cilantro

To make the hummus, if using fresh garbanzos, bring a pot of water to a boil. Fill a bowl with ice water and place it near the stove. Add the garbanzos and garlic to the boiling water and cook for 2 minutes. Drain and transfer to the ice water to cool, then drain again. If using dried garbanzos, pound the cumin seeds in a mortar with a pestle to crack them. Combine the beans and cumin in a saucepan and add water to cover. Bring to a boil, reduce the heat to low, and simmer, partially covered, until the beans are completely soft, 2½ to 3 hours. Remove from the heat and drain.

Put the garbanzos, garlic (if using), tahini, mint (if using fresh garbanzos), lemon juice, and in a food processor. Process until smooth. With the motor on, add olive oil in a steady stream until the hummus has the consistency you like.

Pour ¼ inch of olive oil into a skillet and heat over medium-high heat. Add the bread and fry until deep golden brown and very crisp, about 3 minutes. Turn and fry until deep golden brown and crisp on the second side.

Press the hard-boiled egg through a sieve. Spread the hummus on the fried bread and top with the sardines. Garnish with the sieved egg and chopped cilantro and serve.

CRAB SANDWICH

Inspired by one of the greatest sandwiches ever created—the lobster roll—this is our West Coast version. We use Dungeness crab, native to the Pacific and available beginning in autumn and lasting into spring. Dressed and served on a crispy griddled croissant, we get a different, but equally decadent treat. *Serves 4*

12 to 16 ounces fresh Dungeness crabmeat, picked over for shell fragments

1 small cucumber, peeled, seeded, and finely chopped

1 bunch chervil, stems removed

1 bunch tarragon, stems removed

Grated zest of 1 lemon

2 tablespoons mayonnaise

1 teaspoon whole-grain mustard

1 teaspoon poppy seeds, lightly toasted

4 Croissants (page 160), split and toasted

In a bowl, combine the crabmeat, cucumber, chervil, tarragon, and lemon zest. In small bowl, stir together the mayonnaise and mustard. Add to the crabmeat mixture along with the poppy seeds and turn carefully to combine. Spoon the crab salad onto the bottom half of each croissant. Cover with top halves and serve.

BAY SHRIMP SANDWICH

Popular on the brunch menu at Bar Tartine, this sandwich is a less expensive but no less tasty alternative to the crab sandwich. *Serves 4*

½ head Little Gem lettuce

½ lemon

¾ to 1 pound cooked bay shrimp

½ cup finely chopped fennel bulb

½ cup chopped fennel tops

½ cup finely chopped celery hearts

½ cup finely chopped celery leaves

2 tablespoons mayonnaise

1 tablespoon crème fraîche

2 tablespoons trout roe

4 Croissants (page 160), split and toasted

Salt

Cut the lettuce into a fine chiffonade. Using a mandoline, cut the lemon half into thin slices. In a bowl, combine the lettuce chiffonade, lemon, shrimp, fennel bulb and tops, and celery hearts and leaves. In a small bowl, stir together the mayonnaise and crème fraîche. Add to the shrimp mixture along with the trout roe and turn carefully to combine. Spoon the shrimp salad onto the bottom half of each croissant. Season with salt. Cover with croissant top halves and serve.

KALE CAESAR

Ignacio Mattos, our talented chef friend, introduced us to the pleasure of eating whole leaves of dressed raw kale. Here, we use black kale, also called *cavalo nero, lacinato,* Tuscan kale, or dinosaur kale. The strong greens carry the bold dressing, making the perfect winter bread salad. Eat as much as you like—this Caesar is a healthful one. *Serves 4 to 6*

CAESAR DRESSING
2 lemons
3 cloves garlic
6 olive oil–packed anchovy fillets
1 large egg yolk
Salt
2 cups olive oil

2 pounds black kale, center stems removed, and torn

Croutons (page 193), made from 4 slices day-old Basic Country Bread

⅔ cup grated or shaved aged Parmesan cheese

To make the dressing, grate the zest from 1 lemon. Cut both lemons in half. Place the garlic, anchovies, and lemon zest in a mortar and pound with a pestle to make a thick paste. Add the egg yolk, a pinch of salt, and a squeeze of lemon juice and stir thoroughly to combine. Continuing to stir, pour in ½ cup of the oil drop by drop. The mixture should look smooth and creamy, a sign that you are building a stable emulsion. Continuing to stir, begin adding the oil in a slow stream. The dressing should thicken. Periodically stop pouring in the oil and add a squeeze of lemon. Taste the dressing and add more salt and lemon juice to taste. Add water, a small spoonful at a time, stirring to thin dressing to the consistency of heavy cream.

In a large bowl, combine the kale and croutons. Pour the dressing over the top and toss to coat. Add the Parmesan, toss again, and serve.

TOMATOES PROVENÇAL

Though this classic is often relegated to being a side dish, the magnificent array of heirloom tomatoes we enjoy every summer changes the rules and calls for this favorite to take a prominent place on the table. *Serves 4 to 6*

4 medium-large ripe heirloom tomatoes (about 2 pounds), halved crosswise

Olive oil

Salt

BREAD CRUMBS

2 slices day-old Basic Country Bread (page 45), each about 1 inch thick

1 tablespoon *herbes de Provence*

Grated zest of 1 lemon

¾ cup grated aged Parmesan cheese

3 tablespoons olive oil

Preheat the oven to 475°F. Arrange the tomatoes on a baking sheet, cut-side up. Spoon olive oil onto each tomato half and season with salt. Bake until the tops start to caramelize slightly, about 15 minutes.

Meanwhile, to make the bread crumbs, put the bread in a food processor and pulse to fine crumbs. Add the herbs, lemon zest, Parmesan, and olive oil and pulse to combine.

Remove the tomatoes from the oven and spoon generous amounts of the crumbs onto the tomato halves. Bake until the crumbs are well toasted, about 15 minutes, and serve.

CHILLED CONSOMMÉ WITH SOLDIERS

Set bold against many food memories is a bowl of Gabrielle Hamilton's chilled consommé eaten one hot East Village summer afternoon at her restaurant, Prune. Most people know clear aspics only from photographs in old cookbooks, but this lost staple of haute cuisine is worth reviving. The rich quality of the chicken stock is key to this recipe, both for flavor and to ensure there is enough gelatin so that the aspic will set when cool. The glistening cubes of cold consommé melting on warm toast are powerfully satisfying. Any toast is fine—warm is best. Soldiers are batons of toast, cut to a uniform size, standing firm and straight like soldiers. *Serves 4 to 6*

RICH CHICKEN STOCK

2 tablespoons olive oil

1 yellow onion, roughly chopped

3 carrots, peeled and roughly chopped

2 stalks celery, roughly chopped

1 chicken, about 3 pounds, giblets and liver removed, rinsed and trimmed of excess fat

6 chicken feet, rinsed

4 chicken legs, rinsed

6 sprigs fresh thyme

1 bay leaf

¼ teaspoon salt

Olive oil

4 slices fresh or day-old Basic Country Bread (page 45), each about 1 inch thick

Tender fresh herbs such as sorrel, chervil, tarragon, fennel tops, celery leaves, or basil tips for garnish

To make the stock, heat the oil in a pot over medium heat. Add the onion and carrots and cook, stirring occasionally, until slightly caramelized, about 10 minutes. Add the celery and cook for 5 minutes more. Add the chicken, chicken feet and legs, thyme, bay leaf, salt, and 4 quarts of water. Slowly bring to a simmer while skimming off any impurities that rise to the top. Continue cooking at a low simmer, uncovered and skimming the surface often, for about 1½ hours.

cont'd

Remove the chicken from the pot. Discard the skin and bones from the chicken; reserve the meat for another use such as chicken salad. Strain the stock through a fine-mesh strainer lined with cheesecloth into a large metal bowl. Place the bowl in an ice bath and stir to cool. As the stock cools, the fat will rise to the top. Skim the fat from the surface and discard. Pour the stock into a clean pot and bring to a boil over high heat. Reduce the heat to simmer and cook uncovered until the stock is reduced to roughly 2 quarts, about 1 hour. Strain again into a metal bowl. Place in an ice bath and stir to cool. Pour the stock into a rectangular glass or enamel-lined dish to a depth of ½ to 1 inch. Cover and refrigerate overnight to set. Reserve the remaining stock for a soup base or other uses; store in a covered container in the refrigerator for up to 3 days.

Just before serving, pour ¼ inch of olive oil into a large skillet and heat over medium-high heat. Add the bread and fry until deep golden brown and very crisp, about 3 minutes. Turn and fry until deep golden brown and crisp on the second side. Cut the fried bread into strips about ½ inch wide. Bring the fried bread to the table while still hot.

Unmold the consommé onto a cutting board. Cut into ½- to 1-inch cubes and arrange on chilled plates. Garnish with the herbs and serve with the soldiers.

WHITE GAZPACHO

Linguists still debate the root of *gazpacho*, the name of the famous Spanish soup, citing many sources, from the Arabic for "soaked bread" to the Greek for "little treasure house of edibles." There is no argument that the basic premise of the soup is as old as bread itself. Roman texts describe a cold mash of old bread, vinegar, and olive oil as "drinkable food." The same mash provided sustenance to farmers in feudal Spain.

Gazpacho varies deliciously (and seasonally) across Spain. The white gazpacho, with its base of bread and garlic, predates the more common tomato-based version introduced after the Spanish arrived in the Americas. Traditionally, the red gazpacho is made using bread to thicken as well. Using the red to garnish the white is a winning compromise. *Serves 4 to 6*

WHITE GAZPACHO

2 pounds raw almonds

2 cloves garlic

4 slices day-old Basic Country Bread (page 45), each about ½ inch thick

6 cups water

½ teaspoon salt

1 cup olive oil

¼ cup sherry vinegar

¼ cup lemon juice

RED GAZPACHO GARNISH

2 cups cherry tomatoes, roughly chopped

2 cups seedless red grapes, roughly chopped

1 English cucumber, peeled and roughly chopped

2 tablespoons olive oil

1 tablespoon sherry vinegar

¼ teaspoon salt

Freshly ground pepper

¼ cup fresh mint leaves, chopped

To make the white gazpacho, bring a pot of water to a boil. Add the almonds and garlic and cook for 2 minutes. Drain. If you want a pure white gazpacho, remove the skins from the almonds when they are cool enough to handle and trim the crusts from the bread. Transfer half of the almonds and garlic to a blender. Add half of the bread and water, along with the salt. Blend on high speed until the mixture is thick and smooth. Add half of the oil and blend again. Pass the gazpacho through a strainer into a large bowl. Repeat with the

cont'd

remaining almonds, garlic, bread, water, and oil. Stir in the vinegar and lemon juice. The gazpacho should have the consistency of heavy cream. Stir in more water if it is too thick. Season with salt if needed. Chill the soup in the refrigerator for 3 to 4 hours.

To make the red gazpacho garnish, in a bowl, combine the tomatoes, grapes, and cucumber. Stir in the olive oil, vinegar, salt, pepper to taste, and mint.

To serve, spoon the cold white gazpacho into shallow bowls and top with a few spoonfuls of the red gazpacho.

SOPA DE AJO

Sopa de ajo, or "garlic soup," is a classic Castilian dish. As with gazpacho, preparations of and garnishes for this soup vary across Spain, but the base of garlic and bread is consistent. Most versions are finished with whole eggs or yolks. You can make the stock and croutons in advance, and once these two components are ready, the soup comes together quickly. The croutons, briefly simmered in the broth, gain an ephemeral soft crunch, while the egg yolk enriches the broth. *Serves 4 to 6*

1 quart Rich Chicken Stock (page 223)

3 tablespoons olive oil

1 head garlic, peeled, separated into cloves, and roughly chopped

½ cup dry white wine

2 teaspoons Spanish paprika

Croutons (page 193), made from 3 slices Basic Country Bread

Chopped fresh flat-leaf parsley for garnish

4 to 6 large egg yolks

Pour the stock into a large saucepan and bring to a simmer over medium-high heat.

Heat a large skillet over medium-high heat and add the olive oil. When the oil is shimmering but not yet smoking, add the garlic, reduce the heat to medium-low, and sauté until light golden brown, 30 seconds to 1 minute. Add the wine and cook, stirring, until it evaporates. Add the paprika and sauté with the garlic for 1 minute.

Add the croutons to the skillet and pour in the hot stock. Bring to a boil and simmer for 2 minutes. Remove the pan from the heat. Garnish with the parsley, spoon the egg yolks onto the surface, and serve.

FRENCH ONION SOUP

The original recipe derives from the most basic of quick soups. Onions, always on hand, were fried in duck fat or butter and used to make a savory broth thickened with bread. Here, we use both duck fat and butter with the addition of cream. The onions infuse the cream with flavor, and as it reduces, the milk solids that are left behind caramelize along with the onions. *Serves 4*

6 large yellow onions, cut into slices ¼ inch thick

1 cup heavy cream

1 tablespoon unsalted butter

1 tablespoon duck fat

1 teaspoon salt

2 cups dry white wine

2 quarts Rich Chicken Stock (page 223)

4 slices day-old Whole-Wheat Bread (page 114) or Basic Country Bread (page 45), each ½ to 1 inch thick

5 ounces Gruyère cheese, grated

Combine the onions, cream, butter, duck fat, and salt in a 3-quart sauté pan. Cook, stirring occasionally, over medium heat until the onions are soft and translucent, about 10 minutes. Adjust the heat level so that the onions and cream cook at a slow boil. Spread the onions over the bottom of the pot, raise the heat slightly, and cook the onions without stirring until the bottom of the pot begins to turn brown, about 6 minutes. Stir the onions with a wooden spoon to scrape up the browned residue. Add ½ cup of the wine and deglaze the pot, stirring to loosen any brown bits sticking to the bottom. Continue cooking the onions without stirring until a browned residue forms again, about 6 minutes. Scrape up the browned residue and deglaze the pot with another ½ cup wine. Repeat the process two more times until the onions take on a deep caramel color.

Pour in the stock, bring to a simmer over medium heat, and cook until the broth is well flavored by the caramelized onions, about 15 minutes. Season with salt if needed.

Preheat the oven to 400°F. Arrange the bread in a single layer on a baking sheet. Toast until dry and brittle, about 15 minutes. Ladle the soup into ovenproof bowls, filling them nearly to the rims. Float a piece of toasted bread on each serving. Sprinkle with the Gruyère. Transfer the bowls to the baking sheet and carefully put the sheet in the oven. Bake until the cheese is bubbly and caramelized, 20 to 30 minutes, and serve.

Jambon Buerre Tartine

Ham, butter, bread—these sandwiches stock road-stop stations and supermarkets across France. A more sophisticated version of this combination can be found in wine bars in Paris, eaten as a light lunch or an afternoon snack with a glass of wine. Use the best ham you can find sliced thin. Cut the soft butter as you would cheese, and spread on the bread. Sandwich the ham between buttered slices of the Basic Country Bread (page 45).

NIÇOISE PAN BAGNAT

A *salade niçoise* pressed between bread, this sandwich is ideal for a day at the beach or a long hike. If the sandwich is prepared a day in advance, the bread softens and the flavors develop overnight as the bread is bathed with the dressing.

I tasted my first *pan bagnat* on a day trip with Liz to a tiny island off the coast of Cannes in the French Riviera—Île Saint-Honorat, named for the patron saint of bakers and pastry chefs. Next to the ferry landing, a salty local had set up shop selling tuna sandwiches. He made one for us using a whole split loaf we had brought from Daniel Colin's bakery. We spent the afternoon on an outcropping overlooking the sea, reading and snacking on the giant sandwich in the sun.

The tuna can be poached a few days ahead of time and stored in the refrigerator covered with oil in a sealed container. Good-quality canned tuna is a fine substitution. Assembling the sandwich is straightforward. *Serves 4 to 6*

TUNA CONFIT

2 pounds fresh tuna fillet, at room temperature, cut into thick slices

Salt

Olive oil

3 cloves garlic

3 dried chiles

3 sprigs thyme

3 sprigs marjoram

3 Gypsy peppers

TAPENADE

2 cups niçoise olives, pitted and chopped

Grated zest and juice of 1 lemon

1 teaspoon fresh thyme leaves

¼ teaspoon red pepper flakes

6 to 8 oil-cured anchovy fillets, drained

2 cloves garlic, roughly chopped

2 tablespoons capers, drained and chopped

1 teaspoon sherry vinegar

2 tablespoons olive oil

1 or 2 Baguettes (page 126), halved lengthwise

1 lemon, cut into paper-thin slices

One 4-ounce jar caper berries, drained

½ pound arugula

To make the tuna confit, arrange the tuna slices in a small pot so that they fit snugly in one layer. Season with salt. Pour in enough olive oil to cover the slices by ½ inch. Pound the garlic in a mortar with a pestle. Add to the pot with the chiles, thyme, and marjoram. Set the pan over the lowest heat level and heat until the oil is warm to the touch. The red hue of the fish will change to pinkish

cont'd

gray, an indication that the fish is cooking. Continue cooking the fish gently for 5 minutes over very low heat. Remove from the heat and let stand for 15 minutes. Let the tuna cool in the oil. The tuna will keep in the pot, covered in the oil, for up to 1 week in the refrigerator.

Preheat the oven to 475°F. Place the peppers on a baking sheet and roast until the skin is blistered and blackened, 20 to 25 minutes. Put the hot peppers in a paper bag and let stand for about 8 minutes so that they sweat and their skin loosens. When the peppers are cool enough to handle, remove the charred skin, stems, and seeds. Transfer to a bowl, season with salt, and dress with olive oil.

To make the tapenade, combine the olives, lemon zest and juice, thyme, red pepper flakes, anchovies, garlic, capers, and vinegar in a food processor and pulse to make a coarse paste. Moisten to taste with the olive oil.

Split a baguette in half lengthwise and spread the tapenade on one or both sides. Remove the tuna from the oil, flake it with a fork, and layer evenly over the bread. Layer the roasted peppers, lemon slices, and capers over the fish. Finish by adding a generous amount of arugula. You can add more than you think because the sandwich will be compacted. Serve the sandwich immediately or wrap tightly in parchment paper and then in plastic wrap. Press between two baking sheets, weighting the top one, and let stand for at least 1 hour. Pressing infuses the bread with flavor. If desired, refrigerate overnight.

CLARISE'S MEATBALL SANDWICHES

Once a month at Tartine, a bag of ground beef finds its way into our walk-in refrigerator. Since we don't use the meat for anything on the regular menu, we know that Melissa Roberts is making her mother Clarise's meatball sandwiches for family meal. The garlic-rich pesto spread includes arugula, which adds a sharp note to balance the rich meatballs and sauce. *Serves 1*

PESTO SPREAD

¼ cup finely chopped garlic

¼ cup fresh flat-leaf parsley leaves, finely chopped

¼ cup fresh basil leaves, finely chopped

½ cup finely chopped arugula

¼ cup pine nuts, crushed

3 tablespoons olive oil

2 tablespoons finely grated Parmesan cheese

2 teaspoons lemon juice

¼ teaspoon salt

MEATBALLS

2 tablespoons olive oil

1 large white onion, chopped

1 pound ground beef with at least 20 percent fat

1 pound ground pork

4 large eggs

1 cup whole milk

1 cup grated Romano cheese

¼ cup dry red wine

2 cups Bread Crumbs (page 193), made from day-old Basic Country Bread or Baguette

1 bunch flat leaf parsley, stems removed and leaves chopped

1½ teaspoons salt

½ teaspoon pepper

¼ teaspoon red pepper flakes

TOMATO SAUCE

3 cloves garlic, chopped

Two 16-ounce cans chopped tomatoes

1 loaf Basic Country Bread (page 45) or Baguette (page 126), split

8 ounces provolone cheese, sliced

To make the pesto spread, combine the garlic, parsley, basil, arugula, pine nuts, olive oil, Parmesan, lemon juice, and salt in a food processor and pulse to form a paste. The spread can be made up to 2 days ahead and refrigerated.

To make the meatballs, in a large skillet over medium-low heat, warm the olive oil. Add the onions and sauté until they are translucent and begin to color, about 15 minutes. Remove from the heat and let cool. Combine the beef, pork, eggs,

cont'd

milk, cheese, wine, bread crumbs, parsley, salt, pepper, red pepper flakes, and cooled onions in a large bowl. Using your hands, mix to combine. Form the meat mixture into small balls the size of apricots.

Heat a large skillet over medium heat. Working in batches, add the meatballs, spacing them about ½ inch apart, and sear them without stirring for about 2 minutes. The meatballs will release from the pan when they are sufficiently browned. Continue to cook the meatballs until browned on all sides. Transfer to a plate and cook the remaining meatballs.

To make the tomato sauce, drain the fat from the skillet and place over medium heat. Add the garlic and sauté for about 2 minutes. Add the tomatoes and deglaze the pan, stirring with a wooden spoon to scrape up the browned residue. Bring the tomatoes to a boil and reduce the heat to low. Return the meatballs to the pan and simmer for 20 minutes.

Preheat the oven to 350°F. Spread the top half of the loaf with the pesto spread. Spoon the meatballs and sauce onto the bottom half and top with the provolone slices and then the top half of the loaf. Loosely wrap the sandwich in aluminum foil. Bake until the cheese has melted and the bread is crispy and toasted, about 25 minutes. Let stand for 10 minutes and then unwrap and cut into slices to serve.

BÁNH-MÌ

French colonists brought baguettes and pâté to Vietnam; the Vietnamese created a sandwich all their own. *Bánh-mì* literally means "bread." When ordering a sandwich in a bahn-mi shop, you state your preferred filling following the term *bánh-mì*. This version is an homage to Mary Phan, a cabaret singer and pastry baker who had charge of me when I started my first cooking job at the Four Seasons in Texas. She advised me against a career in the kitchen, telling me I was "not fit for it." She also made for me my first Vietnamese baguette sandwich with the finest ingredients pilfered from the hotel bakeshop and charcuterie kitchen.

This sandwich utilizes leftovers from two other recipes in this book. You can set the components on a table and let everyone make their own. Don't pass on the special garlic fish sauce adapted from John Thorn's recipe—it's essential to capture the authentic flavor of the sandwich. *Serves 4 to 8*

PICKLED VEGETABLES
3 cups red wine vinegar

3 cups water

½ cup sugar

2 tablespoons salt

1 red onion, cut into slices ¼ inch thick

1 bunch small carrots, peeled and cut lengthwise into matchstick strips

1 bunch radishes, thinly sliced

GREEN AIOLI
1 bunch basil, stems removed

1 bunch cilantro, roughly chopped

2 cups Quick Aioli (page 261) or good-quality mayonnaise

3 cloves garlic, if using mayonnaise

Juice of 2 limes

1 jalapeño or serrano chile, seeded

1 teaspoon salt

GARLIC FISH SAUCE
4 cloves garlic

Juice and pulp from 3 limes

1 teaspoon chili oil

2 tablespoons Vietnamese fish sauce

1 or 2 freshly baked or day-old Baguettes (page 126), each halved lengthwise, divided into 4 sections, and toasted

12 slices Porchetta (page 269) or 10 ounces pork-based cold cut such as mortadella or headcheese

Baker's Foie (page 265)

2 limes, cut into quarters

To make the pickled vegetables, in a large bowl, stir together the vinegar, water, sugar, and salt. Add the onion, carrots, and radishes. Let stand for at least 30 minutes. The vegetables will soften slightly, and their color will intensify.

cont'd

To make the green aioli, put 1 cup of the basil and 1 cup of cilantro in a blender. Reserve the remaining herbs for garnish. Add the aioli or mayonnaise, garlic (if using mayonnaise), lime juice, chile, and salt and process until uniformly green and smooth. Add a spoonful of water if the aioli seems too thick.

Just before serving, make the garlic fish sauce. Pound garlic in mortar with pestle to a paste. Add the lime juice and pulp and pound again to a paste. Stir in the chili oil and fish sauce.

Set out serving bowls of the pickled vegetables, green aioli, garlic fish sauce, and reserved herbs. Arrange the toasted baguettes and porchetta on a serving plate with the foie. Assemble sandwiches as you like and garnish with the herbs and a squeeze of lime.

PANADE

Panade is a basic French preparation similar to the Spanish *sopa seca*, or "dry soup." The Italian version is called *ribollita*, and in Macedonia, *paximadia*, or rusks, are used to make the dry soup. The variations are infinite, but the foundation is always dry bread moistened with water or stock and cooked on the stove top or in the oven until the bread has absorbed almost all of the liquid. Root vegetables, cabbage, greens, and other vegetables on hand can be added along with herbs and a piece of smoked meat to flavor the whole. Unlike egg-based bread pudding, which is usually eaten fresh from the oven, this *panade* sets and retains its shape best on the second or third day. It is then cut into wedges, moistened with a spoonful of cream, and reheated. These slices of savory pie are much more handsome than when served straight out of the oven. *Serves 4 to 6*

6 tablespoons unsalted butter

2 leeks, white parts only, finely chopped

6 cups whole milk

Salt

4 slices day-old Basic Country Bread (page 45), each about 1 inch thick

1 small butternut squash (about 1 pound), peeled, seeded, and cut into slices ¼ inch thick

1 bunch black kale, stems removed

1 head cauliflower (about 1½ pounds), trimmed and cut into ½ inch slices

½ pound fontina cheese, thinly sliced

Heavy cream (optional)

Preheat the oven to 375°F.

Melt 1 tablespoon of the butter in a saucepan over medium heat. Add the leeks and sauté until softened, about 5 minutes. Add 2 cups of the milk, the remaining 5 tablespoons butter, and 2 teaspoons salt. Bring to a boil and then remove from the heat.

Cover the bottom of a deep, heavy, 5-quart pot with 2 or more slices of the bread. Arrange the squash slices in an even layer on top of the bread and pour in 2 cups of the hot milk mixture. Top with the remaining 2 bread slices and then with the kale. Arrange the cauliflower slices over the kale. Press the ingredients down to compact them if they don't quite fit into the pot.

cont'd

Pour the remaining 4 cups milk mixture over the vegetables and bread. Stop adding the milk when the level is almost to the rim. Season with salt. Cover the pot with the lid or aluminum foil. Bake for 30 minutes. Uncover and arrange the cheese over the top. Cover, return to the oven, and bake until the liquid is absorbed and reduced, and the cheese has melted and browned, about 20 minutes. When the *panade* has cooled, it should appear dry.

Serve immediately or let cool and refrigerate for up to 3 days. To reheat, cut the panade into wedges and put on individual ovenproof plates. Pour ¼ cup cream over the top of each wedge and bake for 15 to 20 minutes in an oven preheated to 375°F.

NETTLE FRITATINE

Intensely green, nettles have the dangerous beauty of stinging hairs that coat the stems, distinguishing them from other leafy greens. The threat is quickly neutralized by heating or blanching the nettles in boiling water. Unusually high in iron, protein, and calcium, nettles are often described as having a flavor similar to spinach, yet much more earthy and herbaceous. I read a mention of *fritatine*, a classic Sicilian preparation, while researching traditional stale bread dishes. Imagined as a sort of omelette, we used coarse bread crumbs, ample nettles, and just enough egg to bind them. Fried in olive oil and served with a simple tomato sauce, *fritatine* is now a treasured favorite.

You will need about eight ounces of nettle leaves for this recipe—ideally a large pile of leaves that will fill the skillet. Because the uncooked leaves will sting, handle them with tongs or gloves. *Serves 1 or 2*

3 tablespoons olive oil

About 8 ounces nettle leaves

Croutons (page 193), made from 3 slices day-old Basic Country Bread, crushed to make coarse bread crumbs

1 large egg

1½ cups Tomato Sauce (page 255)

Salt and freshly ground pepper

1 lemon wedge

Heat a heavy 12-inch skillet over medium heat and add 1 tablespoon of the olive oil. When the oil is hot but not yet smoking, add the nettle leaves. Remove the pan from the heat, and stir and toss the nettles for about 2 minutes as they continue cooking. When the nettles are completely wilted, remove them from the pan and chop roughly.

In a bowl, combine the nettles, coarse crumbs, and egg. Stir well to coat the crumbs and nettles with the egg.

Heat a 6-inch skillet over medium heat and add the remaining 2 tablespoons of olive oil. When the oil is hot, add the nettle mixture and distribute evenly in the pan. Cook until the edges appear crisp, about 2 minutes. Fold the omelette in half and cook for 30 seconds. Transfer to a plate.

Pour the tomato sauce into the skillet and heat over high heat. Carefully place the omelette in the sauce and simmer for about 30 seconds. Serve with a squeeze of lemon.

LE TOURIN

Le Tourin is a sustenance soup that is at once both food and drink. Eaten across southwest France, it varies according to what's on hand in a given region. This bread soup is prepared quickly and eaten early in the day or midday as a restorative before the afternoon's work. In its simplest form, *le tourin* is made of onions fried in oil or goose fat, boiled in water, and then poured over stale bread and topped with a fried egg seasoned with vinegar. Here, the liquid is enriched with stock, and vegetables are added to make a meal. *Serves 2*

2 tablespoons olive oil or rendered duck or chicken fat, plus ¼ cup

1 bunch young carrots, peeled and cut in half lengthwise

2 yellow onions, cut into quarters

1 bunch kale, stems removed

1 quart Rich Chicken Stock (page 223)

2 large eggs

Salt and freshly ground pepper

Red wine vinegar

3 slices day-old Whole-Wheat Bread (page 114) or Basic Country Bread (page 45), torn into chunks

Place a large sauté pan over medium-high heat and warm the 2 tablespoons olive oil. Add the carrots and onion quarters, cut-side down. Reduce the heat to medium and cook without stirring until slightly caramelized, 5 to 8 minutes. Turn the vegetables, being sure to cook the second cut sides of the onion quarters. Cook until caramelized, 5 to 8 minutes. Add the kale and the stock and bring to a boil. Reduce the heat to simmer and cook for 10 minutes.

Heat a small omelette pan over high heat. Add the ¼ cup olive oil. When the oil is shimmering but not yet smoking, crack the eggs into the pan without breaking the yolks. Fry for about 2½ minutes, carefully spooning some of the hot oil over the eggs to help cook the tops. Carefully pour off the excess oil. Season the eggs with salt, pepper, and vinegar.

Set the torn bread and vegetables in heatproof bowls. Pour the hot stock over the bread and vegetables. Top with the fried eggs and serve.

GARBANZO BREAKFAST SOUP

Late one night, I glimpsed this Tunisian worker's breakfast, called *leblebi*, on a travel documentary. Bowls of garbanzo beans, spices, preserved fish, and dry bread were arrayed in clay vessels on a large table. Workers brought their own utensils and chose how much of each item they wanted. Their bowls were finished with a ladle of hot stock and topped with a soft poached egg. Chermoula, a regional sauce that goes well with most anything, finishes this soup well. *Serves 4 to 6*

6 cups Rich Chicken Stock (page 223)

GARBANZO BEANS

2 pounds fresh garbanzo beans, shelled, or 1 pound dried garbanzo beans

1 teaspoon cumin seeds, if using dried garbanzos

1 yellow onion, roughly chopped, if using dried garbanzos

2 teaspoons salt, if using dried garbanzos

HARISSA

1 Gypsy pepper

4 dried chiles

1 tablespoon cumin seeds

1 teaspoon fennel seeds

1 teaspoon coriander seeds

8 cloves garlic, chopped

¼ teaspoon salt

½ cup olive oil

CHERMOULA

2 shallots, finely chopped

Zest and juice of 2 lemons

2 cloves garlic, finely chopped

1 cup fresh mint leaves, finely chopped

1 cup fresh cilantro leaves and stems, finely chopped

1 tablespoon coriander seeds, toasted and crushed

3 tablespoons cumin seeds, toasted and crushed

1 tablespoon sweet paprika

3 serrano chiles, seeded and finely chopped

½ cup olive oil

Croutons (page 193), made from 6 slices day-old Basic Country Bread or Whole-Wheat Bread

½ to ¾ pounds Tuna Confit (page 233) or two 6-ounce cans olive oil–packed tuna, drained

½ teaspoon salt

4 to 6 eggs

3 tablespoons cumin seeds, toasted and ground, for garnish (optional)

cont'd

Prepare the stock as directed; omit the chicken feet if you like.

If using fresh garbanzos, bring a saucepan with 2 quarts of water to a boil. Add the garbanzos and cook for 2 minutes. Drain. If using dried garbanzos, combine the garbanzos, cumin seeds, onion, and salt in a saucepan and add 2 quarts of water. Bring to a boil, reduce the heat to low, and simmer, partially covered, until the beans are completely soft, 2 to 3 hours. Remove from the heat but do not drain.

To make the *harissa*, preheat the oven to 475°F. Place the pepper on a baking sheet and roast until the skin is blistered and blackened, 20 to 25 minutes. Put the hot pepper in a paper bag and let stand for about 8 minutes so that it sweats and the skin loosens. When the pepper is cool enough to handle, remove the charred skin, stems, and seeds, and roughly chop. Heat a small skillet over high heat. Add the chiles and press down on them with a spatula, and toast for 3 to 5 minutes. Turn the chiles and press with the spatula to toast on the second side for 3 to 5 minutes. Transfer the chiles to a mortar; they will become brittle as they cool. Heat the same skillet over medium heat. Add the cumin, fennel, and coriander seeds and toast, stirring constantly, until you smell the strong toasted aroma, 6 to 8 minutes. Transfer to the mortar. Using a pestle, pound to a fine powder. Add the chopped pepper, garlic, and salt and pound to a thick paste. Pour the olive oil in the same skillet and heat over medium-high heat until it starts to smoke. Turn off the heat, carefully add the garlic-spice paste (it will bubble and sputter), and stir gently with a wooden spoon to disperse the paste. Let the *harissa* cool in the skillet and then transfer to a serving bowl.

To make the *chermoula*, place all the ingredients in a food processor and pulse to make a rough paste.

Right before serving, pour the stock into a saucepan and heat over medium-high heat. Keep warm. Drain the garbanzo beans if necessary. Divide the croutons, garbanzo beans, chermoula, and tuna among serving bowls.

Bring a saucepan with 2 quarts of water to a boil. Add the ½ teaspoon salt and reduce the heat to low. Crack each egg into a small bowl, being careful not to break the yolk. Holding the bowl near the simmering water and tilting it, slide the egg into the water. Cook the eggs until they float to the surface, just under 2 minutes. Use a slotted spoon to remove the eggs from the water.

Ladle the hot stock into the bowls. Place a poached egg in each bowl and garnish with a spoonful of *harissa*. Season with toasted cumin and serve.

INVOLTINI

Involtini, derived from a word meaning "to wrap or bundle," are preparations in which meat, fish, or vegetables are wrapped around a filling that often includes bread crumbs. Depending on the recipe, the rolls are served cold or baked with sauce as we do here. In southern Italy, religious tradition regarding the use of old bread advises one to waste none—a welcome respect for a loaf labored over. *Serves 4 to 6*

TOMATO SAUCE

1 yellow onion, finely chopped

1 carrot, peeled and finely chopped

3 tablespoons olive oil

One 3-ounce can tomato paste

3 cloves garlic, finely chopped

1 teaspoon red pepper flakes

One 16-ounce can whole tomatoes

Red wine vinegar

Salt

STUFFING

Bread crumbs (page 193), made from 4 slices day-old Basic Country Bread, Whole-Wheat Bread, or Semolina Bread

2 cups whole milk ricotta

Grated zest and juice of 1 lemon

1 teaspoon fresh thyme leaves

¼ teaspoon salt

2 or 3 medium globe eggplants

Salt

Olive oil

1 cup heavy cream

½ cup finely grated Asiago cheese

To make the tomato sauce, heat a deep skillet over medium-high heat. Add the onion, carrot, and 2 tablespoons of the olive oil and sauté until the vegetables are soft, about 10 minutes. Add the remaining 1 tablespoon olive oil and the tomato paste and cook, stirring occasionally, until the paste turns a deep rusty red, 6 to 8 minutes. Stir in the garlic and the red pepper flakes and cook for 2 minutes. Add the whole tomatoes, raise the heat to high, and bring to a boil. Reduce the heat to low and simmer for 20 minutes, using a wooden spoon to mash the tomatoes into chunks. Season with vinegar and salt.

Meanwhile, to make the stuffing, in a bowl, stir together the bread crumbs, ricotta, lemon zest and juice, thyme, and salt.

cont'd

Trim the stem end of each eggplant. Using a mandoline, cut the eggplant lengthwise into slices ¼ inch thick. You should have 12 slices. Sprinkle the slices on both sides with salt, layer them in a colander, and let stand for 1 hour. Press the moisture from the eggplant and blot them dry with a kitchen towel. Pour olive oil to a depth of 1 inch in a deep, heavy saucepan or large skillet and heat to 360°F on a deep-frying thermometer. Place 3 or 4 of the eggplant slices in the hot oil and cook until the slices take on some color, 3 to 4 minutes. Using tongs, remove the slices and put in a colander to drain. Repeat with remaining slices.

Preheat the oven to 425°F. Pour the tomato sauce into a medium-sized baking dish. Place a spoonful of filling at the one end of each eggplant slice. Roll the slice around the filling and place it seam-side down in the dish on top of the tomato sauce. Spoon a generous tablespoon of cream over each roll to moisten it. Bake until the edges of sauce around the sides of the dish are dark and the rolls are nicely caramelized, 20 to 25 minutes. Garnish with the Asiago cheese before serving.

SAVORY BREAD PUDDING

This savory pudding has all the aspects you like about a soufflé but is nearly impossible to mess up—it even soufflés when baked. You can assemble the dish up to a day ahead and store it in the refrigerator, letting it come to room temperature before baking. Bake the pudding an hour before you want to serve it. For the mushrooms, we use a mixture of chanterelles and porcini. *Serves 4 to 6*

1 tablespoon unsalted butter

2 leeks, white parts only, finely chopped

½ cup dry white wine

Olive oil

2 pounds assorted mushrooms, stems trimmed and caps halved

1 head Treviso or other radicchio, leaves separated

CUSTARD

5 large eggs

½ teaspoon salt

1 cup heavy cream

1 cup whole milk

¼ teaspoon freshly ground pepper

¼ teaspoon freshly ground nutmeg

2 teaspoons fresh thyme leaves

⅔ cup grated Gruyère or cheddar cheese

3 ounces smoked ham, chopped

2 slices day-old Basic Country Bread (page 45), torn into large chunks

½ cup grated Gruyère or cheddar cheese

Melt the butter in a skillet over medium heat. Add the leeks and sauté until soft, 6 to 8 minutes. Add the wine and cook, stirring occasionally, until most of wine evaporates, about 5 minutes. Remove from the heat.

Heat a large, heavy-bottomed skillet over high heat. Add enough olive oil to coat the bottom of the pan. When the oil is smoking, arrange the mushrooms cut-side down in the pan and cook without stirring until seared and caramelized, about 1 minute more. Stir the mushrooms, add the radicchio, and cook until wilted, about 1 minute. Season to taste. Remove from the heat.

Preheat the oven to 375°F.

cont'd

To make the custard, in a bowl, whisk the eggs and salt until well blended. Add the cream, milk, pepper, nutmeg, thyme, cheese, and ham and whisk to combine.

Place the bread chunks in an 8-inch soufflé dish and add the leeks, mushrooms, and radicchio. Pour in the custard so that it comes all the way to the rim. Sprinkle evenly with the cheese. Let stand for 8 to 10 until the custard saturates the bread.

Bake until the custard is no longer runny in the center, about 50 minutes. Let the pudding rest for 15 minutes before serving.

BURGER

There are countless great burgers out there, but the best ones take the bun seriously. This one includes lots of our favorite things: it is made from grass-fed beef, assembled on a fresh toasted brioche bun which should fit the burger snugly, and piled with toppings. The pickles couldn't be quicker to make. The tomato jam adds a familiar flavor with a sweet, tart balance. Ribbon fries with herbs are a natural companion to the burger. Have someone help by working the fryer while you grill the meat. You can bake the buns and make the caramelized onions and tomato jam up to 3 days ahead. *Serves 6*

BRIOCHE BUNS
6 pieces Brioche dough (page 144), about 115 grams each

2 large egg yolks mixed with 1 tablespoon heavy cream

1 tablespoon poppy seeds

1 teaspoon sesame seeds

CARAMELIZED ONIONS
2 tablespoons unsalted butter

2 red onions, cut into slices ¼ inch thick

½ teaspoon salt

1 tablespoon sherry vinegar

CHERRY TOMATO JAM
6 ounces dry-cured Spanish chorizo, finely chopped

1 shallot, finely chopped

1 pound cherry tomatoes

1 teaspoon fresh marjoram leaves

1 teaspoon fresh thyme leaves

½ cup dried currants, soaked for 5 minutes in warm water, drained, and roughly chopped

2 teaspoons sherry vinegar

½ teaspoon packed brown sugar

¼ teaspoon salt

QUICK AIOLI
1 cup mayonnaise

3 tablespoons extra-virgin olive oil

1 clove garlic, crushed

Grated zest and juice of 1 lemon

QUICK PICKLES
1 English cucumber, cut into slices ⅛ inch thick

2 teaspoons salt

3 tablespoons fresh chopped dill

1 cup rice wine vinegar

½ cup water

FRIED POTATOES
2 pounds russet or Kennebec potatoes, unpeeled

4 cups olive or peanut oil

Salt and freshly ground pepper

1 cup fresh sage leaves

½ cup fresh marjoram leaves

cont'd

BEEF PATTIES

2½ pounds ground grass-fed beef with at least 20 percent fat

1½ teaspoons salt

½ teaspoon freshly cracked pepper

8 ounces Comté cheese, sliced

Unsalted butter, softened

2 avocados, peeled, pitted, and sliced

2 heads Little Gem or iceberg lettuce

To make the buns, start at least 3 hours before serving the burgers. Form each piece of dough into a bun shape. Place the dough shapes on a baking sheet, spacing them 6 inches apart. Press slightly to flatten and spread them a bit. Let rise at moderate room temperature for 1½ to 2 hours. Preheat the oven to 450°F. Brush the dough with the egg wash and top with the poppy and sesame seeds. Bake until the buns are golden brown, about 15 minutes.

To make the caramelized onions, melt the butter in a skillet over medium heat. Add the onions and salt and cook, stirring occasionally, until the onions are soft and translucent, 10 to 15 minutes. Continue cooking the onions without stirring until the bottom of the pan begins to turn brown, about 5 minutes. Stir the onions with a wooden spoon to scrape up the browned residue. Cook the onions for another 5 minutes without stirring until a browned residue forms again and then scrape up the residue. Repeat the process until onions take on a deep caramel color, 10 to 15 minutes. Add the vinegar and deglaze the pan, stirring to scrape up the browned bits, and cook for another minute. Transfer the caramelized onions to a bowl to cool.

To make the tomato jam, evenly distribute the chorizo in the same skillet over high heat. Cook until the chorizo releases some fat, about 5 minutes. Add the shallot and cook until softened, 3 to 5 minutes. Add the cherry tomatoes and cook, stirring occasionally, until the tomatoes pop and release their liquid. Reduce the heat to medium, add the marjoram, thyme, and currants, and cook, stirring frequently, until the liquid has evaporated and the jam is thick, about 15 minutes. Stir in the vinegar, brown sugar, and salt a few minutes before the jam is done. Transfer to a bowl.

To make the aioli, in a bowl, stir together the mayonnaise, olive oil, garlic, and lemon zest and juice. Cover and refrigerate until serving.

To make the pickles, in a bowl, toss the cucumber slices with the salt and dill. Add the vinegar and water. Set aside until serving.

To prepare the fried potatoes, about 1 hour before you plan to cook them, use a mandoline or wide vegetable peeler to cut the potatoes lengthwise into thin, translucent slices about ⅛ inch thick. Stack the slices and cut lengthwise into strips ½ inch wide. Place the strips in a bowl of cold water and set aside to soak for at least 15 minutes or up to 1 hour.

cont'd

To make the beef patties, prepare a fire in a charcoal grill about 30 minutes before serving the burgers. Place the ground beef in a bowl and, using your hands, work the salt and the pepper into the meat. The meat patties shrink as they cook, so shape them ½ to 1 inch larger in diameter than the buns. Sprinkle a little salt over both sides of the patties. Grill the patties for 3 minutes or until done to your preference. Turn the patties, top with the cheese slices and some of the caramelized onions, and grill until the cheese has melted and the burgers are seared on the second side, about 3 minutes. Transfer to a plate and let rest for 2 minutes.

Cut the buns in half and spread the cut sides of both halves with the softened butter. Place the halves on the grill, buttered-side down, and toast until golden brown, about 2 minutes.

Heat the oil in a deep, heavy pot or an electric deep fryer to 375°F on a deep-frying thermometer. Line a plate with paper towels and put near the stove or fryer. Working in small batches, grab a handful of the potatoes and let the water drain off as much as possible. Place the potatoes in the oil; be careful, as the oil level will rise quickly. Fry the potatoes until golden brown, giving a gentle stir, about 3 minutes. Using a strainer, transfer the potatoes to the paper towels. Season with salt and pepper. Repeat the process to cook the remaining potatoes, taking care to let oil return to 375°F. When the potatoes are done, fry the sage and marjoram leaves in the hot oil until crisp, about 10 seconds. Remove and toss with the fries.

Bring the plate of patties, and the grilled buns—along with the tomato jam, aioli, avocados, and lettuce—to the table. Assemble burgers as you like and accompany with fried potatoes.

BAKER'S FOIE

Daniel Colin's Boulangerie Artisanale was in an ancient stone building. The ground floor held a pastry kitchen, a bread workshop, a massive wood-fired oven, and a shop for selling baked goods and prepared foods. Fresh jars of pâté and jam were always on the ledge next to the oven. We spread them on warm bread as a bakers' snack.

I rarely have the time required to make traditional pâtés. So we worked up a quick and delicious recipe that satisfies our pâté cravings. It tastes as if you spent more time and resources than you actually did. The trick is to make sure the butter is at room temperature and the livers have cooled before you blend the two. The pâté is topped with a layer of cognac-infused butter before refrigerating, gilding the baker's foie. *Serves 4 to 6*

6 duck or chicken livers

Olive oil

3 shallots, finely chopped

1 tablespoon fresh thyme leaves

6 tablespoons unsalted butter, at room temperature

½ cup cognac

½ teaspoon salt

COGNAC BUTTER

3 tablespoons unsalted butter, at room temperature

1 tablespoon cognac

Pinch of salt

3 slices Basic Country Bread (page 45) or Whole-Wheat Bread (page 114), toasted

Rinse the livers in cold water and remove any visible fat or connective tissue. Heat a heavy skillet over high heat and add enough olive oil to coat the bottom of the pan. When the oil begins to smoke, carefully add the livers and sear for about 30 seconds. Quickly turn the livers, add the shallots, and sear for another 30 seconds. Add the thyme and cook for a few seconds until it is aromatic. Remove the pan from the heat and pour off the excess oil and fat. While the pan is still hot, add 2 tablespoons of the butter and ¼ cup of the cognac, and deglaze the pan, stirring to loosen any brown bits sticking to the bottom. Transfer the contents of the pan to a food processor and let cool for 8 to 10 minutes.

cont'd

Once the livers have cooled, add the remaining 4 tablespoons butter to the food processor and process to a thick puree. Add the salt and the remaining ¼ cup cognac and process again. Taste and add more salt if needed. Pour the liver puree into ramekins or into a suitably sized loaf or pâté pan.

To make the cognac butter, place the butter in a small bowl. In a small saucepan, heat the cognac until it is hot to the touch. Add it to the butter along with the salt. Stir the butter until it has a liquid consistency and then pour it evenly over the pâté. Cover and refrigerate until the cognac butter has set. Serve cool or at room temperature with toast.

PORCHETTA

Porchetta is a regal way to cook a pork shoulder. Baked for eight hours or longer at a low oven temperature, the meat bastes itself and fills the kitchen with a sublime savory aroma. It's best to prepare this meat the night before you want to serve it. When you take it out of the oven in the morning, you can eat a slice for breakfast with eggs and toast. Serve the *porchetta* with polenta and use leftovers for Bành-Mì sandwiches (page 241). *Serves 4 to 6*

5 pounds boneless pork shoulder

1 teaspoon salt

STUFFING

1 bunch flat-leaf parsley, stems removed

12 fresh sage leaves

1 tablespoon fresh rosemary leaves

2 tablespoons fresh thyme leaves

1 cup fennel tops, chopped

¼ teaspoon red pepper flakes

1 tablespoon fennel seeds

5 cloves garlic

2 teaspoons salt

4 slices day-old Basic Country Bread (page 45), each about 1 inch thick, torn into small chunks

3 tablespoons olive oil

Olive oil

Have your butcher butterfly the pork shoulder to an even thickness of 1 inch. You should have a long sheet of meat roughly 9 by 14 inches. Lay the pork shoulder out flat on a cutting board. Season with 1 teaspoon salt.

Preheat the oven to 220°F.

To make the stuffing, in a food processor, combine the parsley, sage, rosemary, thyme, fennel tops, red pepper flakes, fennel seeds, garlic, and salt, and pulse to chop. Add the bread and olive oil and pulse to combine.

Spread the stuffing evenly over the surface of the meat. Beginning on one side, roll the meat up tight and secure with butcher's twine.

cont'd

Place the roll on a sheet of aluminum foil. Fold the sides of the foil up and around both ends of roast and then roll the roast to enclose it in the foil. This helps retain the moisture and fat while the roast is cooking. Place the roast on a baking sheet and bake until the meat is very tender, 8 to 10 hours.

Leave the aluminum foil on the roast while it cools. Refrigerate for at least 2 hours to allow the roast to firm up and hold its shape.

Remove the roast from the foil and cut off the twine. Cut the roast crosswise into slices about 1 inch thick. Heat a heavy skillet over medium heat. When the skillet is hot, add enough olive oil to cover the bottom of the pan, and add as many slices of porchetta as will fit in the pan. Cook the slices until brown, 3 to 5 minutes. Turn and cook until browned on the second side and heated through, 2 to 4 minutes. Serve.

TARTINE BAKED FRENCH TOAST

When we considered our ideal French toast at the bakery, we imagined a thick slice of our bread set rich with baked custard. The top would be crispy and caramelized like crème brûlée. Though the resulting recipe borrows elements from bread pudding, the results are unmistakably French toast. The bread slices are soaked in the custard base for at least an hour ahead of time, and each slice absorbs more than a cup of liquid. The two large slices will fit in a standard cast-iron skillet, but you can easily double or triple the custard base to make more toasts. In the autumn and winter, we spread the toast with ripe persimmon and eat with bacon and maple syrup. Sautéed apples or pears would be fine stand-ins. *Serves 2*

CUSTARD BASE
3 eggs
2 tablespoons sugar
Zest of 1 lemon
½ teaspoon vanilla extract
¼ teaspoon salt
1 cup milk

2 slices day-old Basic Country Bread (page 45), each about 1½ inches thick
2 tablespoons unsalted butter

MAPLE-GLAZED BACON
4 thick-cut strips bacon
1 tablespoon maple syrup

1 very ripe Hachiya persimmon

To make the custard base, in a bowl, stir together the eggs, sugar, lemon zest, vanilla, salt, and milk.

Place the bread slices in the custard base and let stand until the bread is saturated, about 1 hour.

Preheat the oven to 350°F.

Heat a skillet over medium-low heat. Melt the butter to coat the bottom of the pan. Lift each bread slice from the custard base and place in the pan. Cook the slices for about 3 minutes, occasionally pressing them against the bottom of the pan with a spatula so the bottoms cook evenly. This step seals the bottoms of the slices by cooking the outer layer of custard base. It also prepares the bread for receiving more custard base.

cont'd

Spoon or ladle more custard base into the center of each bread slice. If the liquid leaks out of the bread and onto the skillet, the bread slices are not quite sealed. Continue cooking for 1 minute, pressing the slices slightly to seal. When the slices are full of custard base, carefully transfer the skillet to the middle rack of the oven. Do not turn the toast.

Bake the slices for 12 to 15 minutes and then gently shake the pan. If the custard base is still liquid, continue baking and check again. Depending on the thickness of the slices, the custard may take up to 20 minutes to cook all the way through. The French toast is done when the custard seems solid and each slice appears inflated, as the custard soufflés when fully cooked.

Meanwhile, to cook the bacon, heat a skillet over medium heat. Add the bacon and cook until the strips begin to get crispy around the edges, about 10 minutes. Pour the fat from the pan and add the maple syrup to coat the bacon. Transfer to the oven alongside the toast and bake until the bacon is glazed, about 5 minutes.

Using the spatula, remove the French toast from the skillet and place them, caramelized-side up onto plates. The skillet side should be caramelized and crisp. Spread the French toast with the persimmon and serve with the bacon.

LEAVENED WAFFLES

Using a young leaven in combination with poolish in waffles yields the characteristic depth of flavor gained from fermentation without the strong sourness. The blend of low-gluten flours and cornstarch results in waffles with a tender, crispy texture. If you mix the batter early in the morning, it will be ready by brunch time. Or, you can mix the batter before you go to bed and refrigerate it, covered, until the morning, when you can beat the egg whites and fold them in just before you make the waffles. *Serves 4 to 6*

4 cups leaven (see page 47)

2 tablespoons poolish (see page 128)

2 cups whole milk

1¼ cups all-purpose flour

1¼ cups pastry flour

⅔ cup cornstarch

7 tablespoons sugar

1 tablespoon salt

½ cup unsalted butter, melted, plus more for brushing

6 eggs, separated

3 tablespoons vanilla extract

Place the leaven and poolish in a large bowl. In a saucepan over low heat, warm the milk until just warm. Pour over the leaven and poolish and stir to combine.

Sift the flours and cornstarch into a bowl. Stir in 5 tablespoons of the sugar and the salt. Add the ½ cup melted butter and the egg yolks to the milk mixture. Gradually add the dry ingredients while mixing to incorporate. Cover and let ferment in a warm place (80° to 85°F) for 3 to 5 hours. The longer you let the batter ferment, the stronger the flavor will be.

Just before making waffles, in a bowl, beat the egg whites with the remaining 2 tablespoons of sugar until medium peaks form. Add the vanilla to the batter, stirring to incorporate, and then fold in the whipped egg whites.

Heat a waffle iron or waffle maker according to the manufacturer's instructions and brush with melted butter. Ladle the batter onto the waffle iron and cook until golden brown and crispy, 3 to 5 minutes, depending on the thickness of the waffles and the type of waffle iron or maker. Serve.

TROUBLE AFFOGATO

Trouble Coffee is at Forty-sixth Avenue and Judah, a few blocks from Ocean Beach where Eric and I surfed for most of the year. After cold dawn surf sessions, we headed to Trouble for "the house" restorative: hot coffee, thick-cut cinnamon toast, and a young coconut served with a straw and a spoon–an inspired combination.

Italian *affogato*, meaning "drowned," refers to a scoop of gelato or ice cream with espresso poured over the top. *This* version of *affogato*, one of my favorite desserts, is inspired by "the house" at Trouble. The crunchy bread crumbs contrast with the exceptionally creamy coconut ice cream. Look for young coconuts at Asian or Mexican produce markets. The goat's milk caramel, or *cajeta*, is also sold at Mexican markets. At Tartine, we use Four Barrel coffee–our peerless neighborhood roaster a few blocks from the bakery. *Serves 4 to 6*

COCONUT ICE CREAM
1¾ cups unsweetened shredded coconut
4 cups heavy cream
2 cups whole milk
2 young fresh coconuts
9 large egg yolks
1⅓ cups sugar
1 tablespoon dark rum
1 teaspoon salt

CINNAMON–BROWNED BUTTER BREAD CRUMBS
2 slices day-old Basic Country Bread (page 45), each about 1 inch thick
3 tablespoons unsalted butter
½ cup sugar
1 teaspoon ground cinnamon
⅛ teaspoon salt

½ cup goat's milk caramel
4 to 6 shots hot, freshly pressed Four Barrel espresso

To make the ice cream, preheat the oven to 300°F. Spread the coconut on a baking sheet and toast until light gold, 15 to 20 minutes.

Combine the cream and milk in a large saucepan and bring to a simmer over medium-high heat. Remove from the heat and stir in the toasted coconut. Let infuse for 45 minutes and then strain through a fine sieve. Discard the coconut solids. Return the cream mixture to the saucepan.

cont'd

Trim the husk from each coconut, removing it down to the hard shell. Using the corner of the blade near the base of a chef's knife or cleaver, crack the thin, hard shell and pop the top off the coconut. Drain all the clear liquid, or coconut water, and save to drink or for another use. Using a spoon, scrape the soft coconut flesh from the shell. Chop roughly.

In a bowl, whisk the yolks and sugar. Bring the cream mixture to a simmer over medium heat. Add 1 cup of the hot cream mixture to the yolks and stir quickly to temper. Add another cup and stir again to combine. Pour the cream-yolk mixture into the remaining cream mixture in the saucepan. Reduce the heat to low and cook, stirring, until slightly thickened, 6 to 8 minutes. Strain the custard through a fine-mesh sieve into a bowl. Stir in the rum, salt, and chopped coconut. Cover and refrigerate overnight.

To make the bread crumbs, preheat the oven to 350°F. Line a baking sheet with parchment paper or a nonstick liner. Cut the crusts from the bread slices and tear the slices into small pieces. Melt the butter in a skillet over medium heat and cook until it begins to brown. Remove the pan from the heat, add the bread and sugar, and stir to combine. Stir in the cinnamon and salt. Transfer the bread mixture to the prepared sheet and bake until the sugar and butter coating caramelizes, 20 to 30 minutes. Remove from the oven and let cool. Transfer to a small container and store in the freezer.

Process the chilled coconut mixture in an ice-cream maker according to the manufacturer's instructions. Transfer to a container, fold in the bread crumbs and goat's milk caramel, and serve immediately, scooping the ice cream into bowls or cups and pouring the espresso over the top.

BOSTOCK

Our Bostock is made from toasted brioche bread soaked with an orange-infused syrup, spread with jam and almond cream, topped with sliced almonds, and baked. It is a close relative of the frangipane croissant. At Tartine, we make extra brioche to supply our bostock production. It is the perfect pastry to enjoy with a café au lait or a pot of tea. We like to vary the jams—sometimes using slighty bitter orange marmalade, and other times choosing a sweeter blackberry or tart apricot. *Serves 4 to 6*

ORANGE SYRUP

¼ cup water

¼ cup granulated sugar

1 teaspoon orange blossom water

¼ cup orange juice

Grated zest of 1 orange

2 tablespoons orange liqueur

ALMOND CREAM

1¾ cups sliced almonds

½ cup granulated sugar

Pinch of salt

2 large eggs

½ cup unsalted butter

2 tablespoons brandy

6 slices Brioche (page 144), each about ½ inch thick, toasted

¾ cup orange marmalade, apricot jam, or berry jam

Confectioners' sugar for dusting

To make the orange syrup, in a small saucepan, combine the water, sugar, orange blossom water, and orange juice and zest. Bring to a simmer over medium-high heat, stirring constantly. When the sugar has dissolved, after about 5 minutes, remove from the heat. Stir in the orange liqueur. Let cool to room temperature.

To make the almond cream, combine 1 cup of the sliced almonds, the sugar, and the salt in a food processor and process until finely ground. Add eggs and butter and process to form a paste. Transfer to a bowl and stir in the brandy. Cover and refrigerate for at least 1 hour or up to 3 days.

cont'd

Preheat the oven to 400°F. Arrange the brioche toasts on a baking sheet. Using a pastry brush, thoroughly soak the toasts with the syrup until they are very moist. Spread with a layer of jam about ⅛ inch thick and follow with a layer of almond cream about ¼ inch thick. Top with the remaining ¾ cup sliced almonds. Bake until deep golden brown, 15 to 20 minutes. The almond cream will caramelize, and the almond slices will toast. Dust with confectioners' sugar before serving.

BABAS WITH PROSECCO-POACHED NECTARINES

This version of the classic is based on brioche soaked in a rum syrup. The French use savarin molds to bake the babas into a ring shape. The Italians use muffin-shaped molds. The baked brioche babas absorb the syrup better if made a day ahead and allowed to dry out slightly. You can adjust the amount of rum in the soaker depending on how strong you like it. If you are using brioche dough from the freezer, let it thaw for 30 minutes or until very cold but no longer frozen before shaping. *Serves 4*

BABAS
4 pieces Brioche dough (page 144),
80 grams each

CANDIED PISTACHIOS
1 cup granulated sugar
⅛ teaspoon salt
¼ cup water
1 cup raw pistachios

POACHING LIQUID AND RUM SOAKER
One 750-ml bottle dry prosecco
1 cup granulated sugar
1 vanilla bean, cut in half lengthwise
1 cup dark rum

RICOTTA FILLING
2 cups whole milk ricotta cheese
½ cup dried currants
Grated zest and juice of 1 orange
½ teaspoon vanilla extract
¼ cup granulated sugar

3 ripe nectarines, pitted and cut into wedges
Confectioners' sugar

To make the babas, at least 3 hours ahead of serving, roll each piece of brioche dough into a cylinder and connect the ends to form a crown shape. Place each brioche shape in a buttered savarin or ring mold. Arrange the molds on a baking sheet and let the dough rise at a moderate room temperature for 2 hours.

Preheat the oven to 375°F. Place the pan with the filled molds into the oven. Bake until golden brown, about 20 minutes. Unmold the babas and let cool.

cont'd

To make the candied pistachios, line a baking sheet with parchment paper or a nonstick liner. In a small saucepan, stir together the sugar, salt, and water. Bring to a boil over medium heat; do not stir the mixture. Boil the sugar mixture until it reaches 320°F on a candy thermometer. If you do not have a thermometer, watch for the bubbling to subside and for the liquid to turn light amber. Remove the saucepan from the heat, add the pistachios, and stir to combine. Empty the contents of the saucepan onto the prepared baking sheet and spread out with a wooden spoon. Let stand until just cool enough to touch. Working quickly before the sugar gets hard and brittle, separate the pistachios and transfer to another plate to cool completely.

To make the poaching liquid and soaker, in a saucepan, combine the prosecco and sugar and bring to boil. Using the back of a paring knife or a spoon, scrape the seeds from the vanilla bean halves into the pan. Add the pod to the pan. Reduce the heat to low and simmer for 5 minutes. Pour all but 1 cup of the liquid into a bowl; add the rum to the bowl make the rum syrup. Set aside to cool. Reserve the remaining 1 cup poaching liquid in the pan.

To make the ricotta filling, in a bowl, stir together the ricotta, currants, orange zest and juice, vanilla, and sugar.

Soak the babas in the rum syrup for at least 10 minutes so they are thoroughly saturated. Bring the reserved poaching liquid to a low simmer, add the nectarines, and poach until the fruit is heated through but still holds its shape, 3 to 5 minutes. Remove the babas from rum syrup and arrange in bowls. Spoon the ricotta filling into the centers of the babas. Surround with the nectarines and a spoonful of the poaching liquid. Garnish with the candied pistachios and dust with confectioners' sugar just before serving.

SUMMER PUDDING

A traditional English preparation, this pudding is a straightforward and simple use of bush berries determined by what is in season and most abundant. Weighting the berry-filled, bread-lined molds presses the juice out, which is absorbed by the brioche. As the pudding chills overnight, it sets up into a dessert that can be sliced like a pie or eaten with a spoon. A balance of sweet and tart fruits such as raspberries, blackberries, blueberries, and huckleberries is ideal. *Serves 4 to 6*

4 cups soft summer berries such as raspberries, blackberries, blueberries, and/or huckleberries

⅔ cup granulated sugar

8 to 10 slices Brioche (page 144), each about ¼ inch thick

1 cup heavy cream, lightly whipped

1 teaspoon confectioners' sugar

In a saucepan over medium heat, combine the berries and the sugar and bring to a boil, stirring constantly. Cook for 1 minute and remove from heat. Line a medium-sized glass or ceramic bowl or 4 to 6 small soup bowls or cups with the brioche slices. Reserve enough slices or pieces of brioche to cover the top(s). Pour the berries and juice into the mold(s). Reserve 2 tablespoons of the berry juice for serving.

Cover the berries with the reserved brioche. Place a plate on top of each mold and weight with cans (of soup, for example) and refrigerate overnight.

Unmold the pudding(s) onto a cutting board or serving platter, or spoon out portions into bowls. Top with the reserved berry juice and the whipped cream. Dust with the confectioners' sugar and serve.

LIZ'S JAM

Liz and I find that making jam is among the most satisfying projects you can do in the kitchen. Jam is preserved proof of a good crop of fruit. It is also versatile—whether served on a cheese plate or as accompaniment to a roast or spread on freshly baked bread or toast.

Jams need three ingredients to set properly: pectin, sugar, and acid. Fruit naturally contains pectin, a jelling agent, in an amount that varies from one type of fruit to another. The fruit you choose must be ripe, but be sure that 25 percent is slightly underripe, as this contains more pectin. Sugar activates the pectin, sweetens the jam, and provides an acidic environment that retards the growth of bacteria. You can use white cane sugar or organic "tan" sugar. Darker organic sugars, which are less refined, will give the jam a different flavor than all-white sugar. Traditional recipes tend to call for a ratio of 1 part fruit to 1 part sugar. These proportions make a very sweet jam with more syrup and fewer fruit solids. The recipe here uses less sugar, which results in a thicker jam. Acid is added in the form of lemon juice.

If you are making jam with low-pectin fruits, you can combine them with a majority of high-pectin fruit. Or, you can add apple to boost the pectin. For each 500 grams of low-pectin fruit, use 1 large unpeeled apple. Cut the apple, including the core, into 1-inch pieces, place on a square of cheesecloth, bring up the corners, and tie firmly with kitchen string. Cook the apple along with the fruit and discard the cheesecloth bundle before ladling the jam into jars.

Jam should be cooked until it reaches 221°F. For every 1,000 feet above sea level, subtract 2°F. For example, if your kitchen is 2,000 feet above sea level, cook the jam until it is 217°F.

High-Pectin Fruits

Apples
Berries: blackberries, boysenberries, gooseberries, loganberries, raspberries
Citrus: oranges, tangerines, grapefruit, lemons including Meyer, limes, kumquats
Concord grapes
Quince

Low-Pectin Fruits

Berries: blueberries, strawberries
Figs
Italian plums
Pears
Stone fruits: apricots, cherries, nectarines, peaches

Basic Jam Recipe

1 kilogram (1,000 grams) fruit
750 grams sugar
Juice of 1 large or 2 small lemons

Wash jars and their lids and metal screw bands in hot soapy water and rinse thoroughly with very hot water. Jam yield varies depending on which fruit and how much sugar you use. Three and a half pounds of fruit, in general, will yield ten 8-ounce jars. To sterilize the jars, place them upright in a large pot, add hot water to cover the jars, bring to a boil, and boil for 15 minutes. Place the lids and bands in a saucepan, add hot water to cover, bring to a boil, and boil for 15 minutes. Also wash the utensils you'll need—wooden spoon, ladle, canning funnel, and jar lifter—and rinse with hot water. Remove the jars, lids, and bands from the boiling water and set aside on a clean work surface.

Wash the fruit and remove any stems or leaves. Cut the fruit into ½- to 1-inch pieces or slices. Combine the fruit, sugar, and lemon juice in a nonreactive pot, making sure that the fruit is 3 inches below the rim of the pot. If you are using fruit that is on the drier side, such as apricots, start by pouring ½ cup water per 500 grams of fruit into the pot. Cook the fruit over medium heat, stirring, until the fruit starts to release its juices and the sugar begins to dissolve.

Raise the heat to high and continue to cook the fruit, stirring as needed to prevent the fruit from sticking to the bottom of the pot. When foam starts to form on the top of the fruit, skim it off with the ladle or wooden spoon. The jam will bubble vigorously at first and then will bubble more slowly. When the jam reaches 220° to 222°F on a thermometer, turn off the heat and wait a few minutes for the temperature to come down a few degrees. If the jam is put immediately into jars, the fruit will float to the top of the syrup. The temperature to which jam is cooked is the same for all fruits and all types of preserving: 221°F at sea level. For every 1,000 feet above sea level, subtract 2°F.

Using the funnel and ladle, fill jars to within ⅛ inch of the rims. Remove any drips with a clean towel. Top with the lids and seal with the screw bands.

If processing the jars in a boiling-water bath, place a rack in a large pot; the surface of the rack should be ¾ to 1 inch above the bottom of the pot. Fill the pot with water and bring to a boil. (If using a purchased canner, follow the manufacturer's instructions.) Using a jar lifter, lower the filled jars into the water, spacing them 1 inch apart and making sure that the jars are covered by 2 inches of water.

Adjust your processing times according to altitude. Most charts are formulated for altitudes of 1,000 feet or less. You must increase the processing time by five minutes for altitudes of 1,000 to 3,000 feet, ten minutes for 3,000 to 6,000 feet, and fifteen minutes for altitudes of 6,000 to 8,000 feet.

Remove the jars from the boiling-water bath and set aside. While the jars cool, the lids will make a popping sound as they contract. This indicates that you have a good vacuum seal.

If the jars have not been processed or have not sealed properly, store in the fridge for up to 6 weeks. Jars of jam that have been properly vacuum sealed will keep in a cool, dark place for at least a year. Check to make sure that the vacuum seal is intact before opening for the first time.

ACKNOWLEDGMENTS

To the hands that inspire good work: My wife and partner Elisabeth; kitchen manager and right hand Melissa; lead bread baker Nathan; multilinguist bread baker Lori; our cafe managers Suzanne, Sierra, and Tahlia; and everyone I work with. Support drawn from my Tartine family is immeasurable. Warmest thanks to you all—and to Mom and Dad always.

Thanks to David Wilson for beautifully illustrating our place and state of mind.

Sincere thanks to Katherine Cowles, for keeping my efforts pointed in the right direction to enable this project. And to Olga Katsnelson and Kate Goldstein-Breyer of Postcard Communications.

Thanks to the editorial team at Chronicle Books: Bill LeBlond, Sarah Billingsley, and Judith Dunham along with Peter Perez and David Hawk. And special thanks to Vanessa Dina. Your dedicated work is much appreciated.

And thanks to Eric, for building this book from start to finish with me; and for capturing so well the record of a special time.

—*Chad Robertson*

My thanks to Chad for inviting me to the shaping table and including me on this project.

My work is dedicated to those whose example keeps me pursuing my dreams,and whose affection, good advice and unwavering support helped make this one possible. Jaz, Marko, Mom, and Dad.

—*Eric Wolfinger*

Index

A

Aioli, 196
    Green Aioli, 241–42
    Quick Aioli, 261–62
Almonds
    Almond Cream, 281
    Bostock, 281–82
    White Gazpacho, 225–27
Anchovies
    Anchoïade, 187–88
    Bagnet Vert, 189–91
    Caesar Dressing, 218
    Marinated Anchovies, 189
    Tapenade, 233–35
Apricots
    Kugelhopf, 156–59
Artichokes
    Roasted Artichoke Croutons, 183–85
    Tomato Panzanella, 183–85
Autolyse, 73

B

Babas with Prosecco-Poached Nectarines, 283–85
Bacon
    Brioche Lardon, 155–56
    Maple-Glazed Bacon, 271–73
Bagnet Vert, 189–91
Baguettes, 126–34
Baker's Foie, 265–67
Baker's percentages, 48
Bánh-Mì, 241–42
Basic Country Bread
    baking, 65–68, 77–79
    bench rest for, 56, 75–76
    bulk fermentation for, 52–55, 74–75
    cooling, 68, 79
    equipment for, 43
    final rise for, 58, 77
    ingredients for, 47–48, 70–71
    leaven for, 47, 72–73
    mixing dough for, 47–52
    process for, 45–68
    rest period for, 52, 73–74
    shaping, 56–58, 75–76
    starter for, 43, 45–46
    test bakers for, 80–87
    variations on, 87–103
Bay Shrimp Sandwich, 217

Beans
    Fresh Fava Panzanella, 181
    Garbanzo Breakfast Soup, 251–53
    Hummus, 213
Beef
    Burger, 261–64
    Clarise's Meatball Sandwiches, 237–39
Beignets, 152–54
Berries
    Summer Pudding, 287
Bostock, 281–82
Bourdon, Richard, 20, 77, 113
Bread. *See also individual recipes*
    baking, 65–68, 77–79
    bench rest for, 56, 75–76
    bulk fermentation for, 52–55, 74–75
    cooling, 68, 79
    equipment for, 43
    final rise for, 58, 77
    history of, 15, 124–26
    ingredients for, 47–48, 70–71
    kneading, 54
    leaven for, 47, 72–73
    mixing dough for, 47–52
    with natural leaven vs. yeast, 15, 124–26
    rest period for, 52, 73–74
    shaping, 56–58, 75–76
    starter for, 43, 45–46
    in wood-fired ovens, 31–32
Bread crumbs, 192, 193
Brioche, 144–49
    Brioche Buns, 261–62
    Brioche Lardon, 155–56
    Olive Brioche, 151–52
Bruschetta
    Eggplant and Charred Pepper Bruschetta, 204
    Late Summer Bruschetta, 201
    Summer Squash and Pea Bruschetta, 203
    Tomato, Melon, and Chile Bruschetta, 202
Buns, Brioche, 261–62
Burger, 261–64
Butter, Cognac, 265–67

C

Caesar Dressing, 218
Calvel, Raymond, 73, 125
Candied Pistachios, 283–85
Caramelized Onions, 261–62

Carrots
  Le Tourin, 248
  Pickled Vegetables, 241–42
Cauliflower
  Panade, 243–45
Cheese
  Babas with Prosecco-Poached Nectarines, 283–85
  Burger, 261–64
  Clarise's Meatball Sandwiches, 237–39
  French Onion Soup, 231
  Involtini, 255–56
  Kale Caesar, 218
  Margherita Pizza, 100
  Nettle Pizza, 95–96
  Pain au Gruyère, 117
  Panade, 243–45
  Pan con Tomate, 199
  Potato Focaccia, 101–3
  Raclette, 206
  Savory Bread Pudding, 257–59
  Summer Squash and Pea Bruschetta, 203
  Tomatoes Provençal, 221
  Tomato Panzanella, 183–85
Chermoula, 251–53
Cherry Tomato Jam, 261–62
Chicken
  Baker's Foie, 265–67
  Bánh-Mì, 241–42
  Chilled Consommé with Soldiers, 223–24
  Rich Chicken Stock, 223–24
Chiles
  Chermoula, 251–53
  Chile Salt, 202
  Harissa, 251–53
  Tomato, Melon, and Chile Bruschetta, 202
Chilled Consommé with Soldiers, 223–24
Chorizo
  Cherry Tomato Jam, 261–62
Clarise's Meatball Sandwiches, 237–39
Coconut
  Coconut Ice Cream, 277–79
  Trouble Affogato, 277–79
Coffee
  Trouble Affogato, 277–79
Cognac
  Baker's Foie, 265–67
  Cognac Butter, 265–67

Colin, Daniel, 22–23, 71, 113, 233, 265
Consommé, Chilled, with Soldiers, 223–24
Country Rye Bread, 118
Crab Sandwich, 215
Croissants, 144, 160–70
Croutons, 193
  Roasted Artichoke Croutons, 183–85
Cucumbers
  Quick Pickles, 261–62
  Tomato Panzanella, 183–85
  White Gazpacho, 225–27
Currants
  Babas with Prosecco-Poached Nectarines, 283–85
  Cherry Tomato Jam, 261–62
  Kugelhopf, 156–59

E
Eggplant
  Eggplant and Charred Pepper Bruschetta, 204
  Escalivada, 187–88
  Involtini, 255–56
Eggs
  Garbanzo Breakfast Soup, 251–53
  Le Tourin, 248
English Muffin, 140–43
Equipment, 43
Escalivada, 187–88

F
Fava Panzanella, Fresh, 181
Fendu, 137–39
Fennel
  Bay Shrimp Sandwich, 217
  Porchetta, 269–70
Figs
  Anchoïade, 187–88
  Escalivada, 187–88
Fish. *See also* Anchovies
  Garbanzo Breakfast Soup, 251–53
  Niçoise Pan Bagnat, 233–35
  Pickled Sardines, 209–11
  Sardines and Fresh Garbanzo Hummus, 213
  Tuna Confit, 233–35
Flax and Sunflower Bread, 116
Flour, 70
Focaccia, Potato, 101–3
Fougasse, 139–40

French Onion Soup, 231
French Toast, Tartine Baked, 271–73
Fresh Fava Panzanella, 181
Fried Potatoes, 261–64
Fruits. *See also individual fruits*
    Liz's Jam, 291–93

G
Garbanzo beans
    Garbanzo Breakfast Soup, 251–53
    Hummus, 213
Garlic
    Garlic Fish Sauce, 241–42
    Sopa de Ajo, 228
Gazpacho, White, 225–27
Golden Raisin, Fennel Seed, and Orange Zest
    Bread, 112
Grapes
    White Gazpacho, 225–27
Green Aioli, 241–42

H
Ham
    Jambon Beurre Tartine, 232
    Pan con Tomate, 199
    Savory Bread Pudding, 257–59
Hamilton, Gabrielle, 223
Harissa, 251–53
Hazelnuts
    Brioche Lardon, 155–56
Herb Salad, 209–11
Hummus, 213
Hydration percentage, 48

I
Ice cream
    Coconut Ice Cream, 277–79
    Trouble Affogato, 277–79
Involtini, 255–56

J
Jambon Beurre Tartine, 232
Jams
    Cherry Tomato Jam, 261–62
    Liz's Jam, 291–93

K
Kale
    Kale Caesar, 218
    Le Tourin, 248
    Panade, 243–45
Krupman, Jeff, 100
Kugelhopf, 156–59

L
Late Summer Bruschetta, 201
Leaven
    aroma of, 73
    characteristics of, 72
    history of, 15, 124–26
    making, 47
    readiness of, 73
    replenishing, 73
    starter and, 71–72
Leavened Waffles, 275
Lemons
    Lemon Glaze, 153–54
    Lemon Vinaigrette, 181, 202
LePort, Patrick, 22, 23, 71, 113
Le Tourin, 248
Liver
    Baker's Foie, 265–67
    Bánh-Mì, 241–42
Liz's Jam, 291–93

M
Maple syrup
    Maple-Glazed Bacon, 271–73
    Maple Pecans, 153–54
Margherita Pizza, 100
Marinated Anchovies, 189
Mattos, Ignacio, 218
Meatball Sandwiches, Clarise's, 237–39
Melons
    Summer Squash and Pea Bruschetta, 203
    Tomato, Melon, and Chile Bruschetta, 202
Mushrooms
    Savory Bread Pudding, 257–59

N

Nectarines, Prosecco-Poached, Babas with, 283–85

Nettles
  Nettle Fritatine, 247
  Nettle Pizza, 95–96

Niçoise Pan Bagnat, 233–35

O

Olives
  Olive Bread, 88
  Olive Brioche, 151–52
  Tapenade, 233–35

Onions
  Caramelized Onions, 261–62
  French Onion Soup, 231
  Le Tourin, 248
  Pickled Vegetables, 241–42

Oranges
  Bostock, 281–82
  Orange Syrup, 281

Oyamada, Lori, 80

P

Pain au Gruyère, 117

Panade, 243–45

Pan con Tomate, 199

Panzanella
  Fresh Fava Panzanella, 181
  Tomato Panzanella, 183–85

Pea and Summer Squash Bruschetta, 203

Pecans, Maple, 153–54

Pepin, Jacques, 15

Peppers. *See also* Chiles
  Eggplant and Charred Pepper Bruschetta, 204
  Escalivada, 187–88
  Harissa, 251–53
  Niçoise Pan Bagnat, 233–35
  Rouille, 196

Pesto Spread, 237

Phan, Mary, 241

Pickles
  Pickled Sardines, 209–11
  Pickled Vegetables, 241–42
  Quick Pickles, 261–62

Pistachios
  Babas with Prosecco-Poached Nectarines, 283–85
  Candied Pistachios, 283–85
  Kugelhopf, 156–59

Pizzas
  Margherita Pizza, 100
  Nettle Pizza, 95–96

Polenta Bread, 93

Poolish, 125

Porchetta, 269–70

Pork
  Bánh-Mì, 241–42
  Cherry Tomato Jam, 261–62
  Clarise's Meatball Sandwiches, 237–39
  Porchetta, 269–70

Potatoes
  Fried Potatoes, 261–64
  Potato Focaccia, 101–3

Prueitt, Elisabeth, 20

Puddings
  Savory Bread Pudding, 257–59
  Summer Pudding, 287

Q

Quick Aioli, 261–62

Quick Pickles, 261–62

R

Raclette, 206

Radicchio
  Savory Bread Pudding, 257–59

Radishes
  Pickled Vegetables, 241–42

Raisins
  Golden Raisin, Fennel Seed, and Orange Zest Bread, 112
  Raisin and Coriander Bread, 116–17

Rich Chicken Stock, 223–24

Roasted Artichoke Croutons, 183–85

Roberts, Melissa, 177, 237

Rouille, 196

Rum
  Babas with Prosecco-Poached Nectarines, 283–85

Rye Bread, Country, 118

S

Salad dressings
  Caesar Dressing, 218
  Lemon Vinaigrette, 181, 202
  Sherry Vinaigrette, 204
Salads
  Escalivada, 187–88
  Fresh Fava Panzanella, 181
  Herb Salad, 209–11
  Kale Caesar, 218
  Tomato Panzanella, 183–85
Salt, 71
Sandwiches
  Bánh-Mì, 241–42
  Bay Shrimp Sandwich, 217
  Burger, 261–64
  Clarise's Meatball Sandwiches, 237–39
  Crab Sandwich, 215
  Jambon Beurre Tartine, 232
  Niçoise Pan Bagnat, 233–35
Sardines
  Pickled Sardines, 209–11
  Sardines and Fresh Garbanzo Hummus, 213
Sauces
  Aioli, 196
  Anchoïade, 187–88
  Bagnet Vert, 189–91
  Chermoula, 251–53
  Garlic Fish Sauce, 241–42
  Green Aioli, 241–42
  Harissa, 251–53
  Hummus, 213
  Quick Aioli, 261–62
  Rouille, 196
  Tomato Sauce, 237–39, 255
Savory Bread Pudding, 257–59
Schwertner, Amaryll, 155–56
Scott, Alan, 26, 77
Semolina flour
  Golden Raisin, Fennel Seed, and Orange Zest Bread, 112
  Semolina Bread, 110–12
Sesame Bread, 90
Sherry Vinaigrette, 204
Shrimp Sandwich, Bay, 217
Sopa de Ajo, 228

Soups
  French Onion Soup, 231
  Garbanzo Breakfast Soup, 251–53
  Le Tourin, 248
  Sopa de Ajo, 228
  White Gazpacho, 225–27
Spreads
  Almond Cream, 281
  Pesto Spread, 237
  Tapenade, 233–35
Squash
  Panade, 243–45
  Summer Squash and Pea Bruschetta, 203
Starter
  acid load of, 72
  leaven and, 71–72
  making, 45–46
  refreshing, 72
  role of, 72
  storing, 72
Steingarten, Jeffrey, 79
Stock, Rich Chicken, 223–24
Summer Pudding, 287
Summer Squash and Pea Bruschetta, 203
Sunflower and Flax Bread, 116
Syrup, Orange, 281

T

Tapenade, 233–35
Tartine Baked French Toast, 271–73
Test bakers, 80–87
Thorn, John, 241
Tomatoes
  Cherry Tomato Jam, 261–62
  Clarise's Meatball Sandwiches, 237–39
  Escalivada, 187–88
  Involtini, 255–56
  Margherita Pizza, 100
  Nettle Fritatine, 247
  Pan con Tomate, 199
  Tomatoes Provençal, 221
  Tomato, Melon, and Chile Bruschetta, 202
  Tomato Panzanella, 183–85
  Tomato Sauce, 237–39, 255
  White Gazpacho, 225–27
Tordu, 137
Trouble Affogato, 277–79

Tuna
    Garbanzo Breakfast Soup, 251–53
    Niçoise Pan Bagnat, 233–35
    Tuna Confit, 233–35

V

Vegetables. *See also individual vegetables*
    Pickled Vegetables, 241–42
Vinaigrettes. *See Salad dressings*

W

Waffles, Leavened, 275
Walnuts
    Anchoïade, 187–88
    Walnut Bread, 91
Water, 71
Waters, Alice, 192
Weiner, Sarah, 144
White Gazpacho, 225–27
Whole-wheat flour
    Flax and Sunflower Bread, 116
    Pain au Gruyère, 117
    Raisin and Coriander Bread, 116–17
    Whole-Wheat Bread, 113–14
Wolfinger, Eric, 11, 13

Y

Yanko, Nate, 80

Z

Zucchini. *See Squash*

Table of Equivalents

The exact equivalents in the following tables have been rounded for convenience.

LIQUID/DRY MEASUREMENTS

U.S.	Metric
¼ teaspoon	1.25 milliliters
½ teaspoon	2.5 milliliters
1 teaspoon	5 milliliters
1 tablespoon (3 teaspoons)	15 milliliters
1 fluid ounce (2 tablespoons)	30 milliliters
¼ cup	60 milliliters
⅓ cup	80 milliliters
½ cup	120 milliliters
1 cup	240 milliliters
1 pint (2 cups)	480 milliliters
1 quart (4 cups, 32 ounces)	960 milliliters
1 gallon (4 quarts)	3.84 liters
1 ounce (by weight)	28 grams
1 pound	448 grams
2.2 pounds	1 kilogram

LENGTHS

U.S.	Metric
⅛ inch	3 millimeters
¼ inch	6 millimeters
½ inch	12 millimeters
1 inch	2.5 centimeters

OVEN TEMPERATURE

Fahrenheit	Celsius	Gas
250	120	½
275	140	1
300	150	2
325	160	3
350	180	4
375	190	5
400	200	6
425	220	7
450	230	8
475	240	9
500	260	10